TRANSLATIONS OF EARLY DOCUMENTS

SERIES II

HELLENISTIC-JEWISH TEXTS

THE LETTER OF ARISTEAS

THE LETTER OF ARISTEAS

TRANSLATED
WITH AN APPENDIX OF ANCIENT EVIDENCE
ON THE ORIGIN OF THE SEPTUAGINT

BY

H. St. J. THACKERAY, M.A.

GRINFIELD LECTURER ON THE SEPTUAGINT IN THE UNIVERSITY OF OXFORD

Wipf and Stock Publishers
EUGENE, OREGON

Wipf and Stock Publishers
199 West 8th Avenue, Suite 3
Eugene, Oregon 97401

The Letter of Aristeas
By H. St. Thackeray, J.
ISBN: 1-59244-172-6
Publication date: March, 2003
Previously published by Society for Promoting Christian Knowledge,
January, 1918 .

EDITORS' PREFACE

THE object of this series of translations is primarily to furnish students with short, cheap, and handy text-books, which, it is hoped, will facilitate the study of the particular texts in class under competent teachers. But it is also hoped that the volumes will be acceptable to the general reader who may be interested in the subjects with which they deal. It has been thought advisable, as a general rule, to restrict the notes and comments to a small compass; more especially as, in most cases, excellent works of a more elaborate character are available. Indeed, it is much to be desired that these translations may have the effect of inducing readers to study the larger works.

Our principal aim, in a word, is to make some difficult texts, important for the study of Christian origins, more generally accessible in faithful and scholarly translations.

In most cases these texts are not available in a cheap and handy form. In one or two cases texts have been included of books which are available in the official Apocrypha; but in every such case reasons exist for putting forth these texts in a new translation, with an Introduction, in this Series.

W. O. E. OESTERLEY.
G. H. BOX.

INTRODUCTION

CONTENTS

THE document known as the Letter of Aristeas purports to be a contemporary record, by a Greek holding a high position at the court of Ptolemy Philadelphus (285–247 B.C.), of the translation of the Hebrew Pentateuch into Greek, undertaken at the instance of the royal librarian, Demetrius of Phalerum. The familiar name "the Septuagint," by which the Greek Old Testament as a whole came to be known, owes its origin to the story here told of the seventy-two translators of the Law. The narrative is communicated in the form of a letter from Aristeas to his brother Philocrates. Aristeas claims to have been a member of the embassy sent from Alexandria to Jerusalem to obtain a copy of the Law and the services of a company of Palestinian translators. The letter is discursive, ranging over a variety of topics; the description of the actual work of translation being compressed into the closing sections. The following is an analysis of the contents :—

I. Introductory address to Philocrates, §§ 1–8.

II. The origin of the scheme and preliminary proceedings, §§ 9–51.

- (*a*) The proposal of the king's librarian, §§ 9–11.
- (*b*) The emancipation of the Jewish slaves in Egypt, §§ 12–27.

(*c*) The librarian's memorial, §§ 28–33.
(*d*) The correspondence between Ptolemy and Eleazar, with the names of the translators, §§ 34–51.

III. Description of the royal presents to Eleazar, §§ 51–82.

IV. Description of Jerusalem and its vicinity, §§ 83–120.
(*a*) The temple: entrance, veil, altar, §§ 84–87.
(*b*) The temple water supply, §§ 88–91.
(*c*) The priests and the public services, §§ 92–95.
(*d*) The high priest's vestments, §§ 96–99.
(*e*) The citadel and its guards, §§ 100–104.
(*f*) The city and its streets, §§ 105–106.
(*g*) Small and large cities—Jerusalem and Alexandria—contrasted, §§ 107–111.
(*h*) The country and its produce: harbours, rivers, mountain ranges, §§ 112–118.
(*i*) The mines of Arabia, §§ 119–120.

V. Eleazar's farewell to the translators, §§ 120–127.

VI. Eleazar's apology for the Jewish Law, §§ 128–171.

VII. Reception of the translators at Alexandria, §§ 172–181.

VIII. The seven days' banquet in honour of the translators, §§ 182–186.

IX. The wise answers of the translators to the king's hard questions, §§ 187–300.

X. The translation and its reception, §§ 301–316.

XI. The departure of the translators, §§ 317–321.

XII. Concluding address to Philocrates, § 322.

Character, Date and Credibility of the Narrative

That the Letter is not what it professes to be, a contemporary record of a Greek who played a prominent part in the actions described, has long been recognized. In various ways the writer betrays himself.

He was not a contemporary of Ptolemy Philadelphus. On two occasions he momentarily forgets his *rôle* and reveals the interval of time which has elapsed since the age of that monarch. He alludes to the scrupulous care with which "all business used to be transacted by these kings" (§ 28), as though he were looking back over an epoch of a long dynasty of Ptolemies. Again, he tells us that the arrangements made at the Alexandrian court for the entertainment of foreigners "may still be seen to this day" (§ 182).

He is not a veracious historian. Where his references to historical characters and events are open to control, he is found guilty of anachronisms and inaccuracies. He represents Demetrius, who, as we learn from other sources, was banished from Alexandria early in the reign of Philadelphus, as the king's confidential friend and librarian, upon whose initiative the translation was undertaken. We have no other evidence that the philosopher Menedemus of Eretria (§ 201) ever visited Alexandria. In the allusion to a naval victory of Ptolemy over Antigonus Gonatas (§ 180) either a decisive defeat of the Egyptian navy at the battle of Cos (*c.* 260 B.C.) has been transformed into a victory, or the reference is to an actual victory at Andros many years later (*c.* 245 B.C.); in either case there is anachronism, both battles having occurred long after the death of Demetrius. The statements with regard to Theopompus (§ 314) and Theodectes (§ 316) are doubtless equally untrustworthy. The writer himself in one place anticipates the incredibility with which his story will be received, and finds it necessary to appeal to the unimpeachable evidence of his authorities (§§ 296 ff.).

Finally—and this is the main count in the indictment—the whole tone of the book proclaims the writer to be a Jew and not, as he would have us believe (§ 16), a Greek. The apologetic tendency is manifest throughout. His main object is to commend and magnify the Jewish nation, with its laws and institutions, in the eyes of the Greek public for which he writes, by narrating the honour bestowed upon it by a Greek monarch and the praise accorded to Jewish wisdom by heathen philosophers (§§ 200 f., 235). He is at pains to explain the absence of any mention of the Jewish Law in the Greek historians and poets (§§ 31, 312 ff.) The apologetic tendency is most apparent in the long exposition given by Eleazar of "the natural (or 'inward') meaning of the Law" (§ 171) with regard to clean and unclean food: a section which is penned with the intention of satisfying a supposed wide-spread "curiosity" (§ 128) and counteracting fallacious and long "exploded" views on the subject (§ 144).

The book, in short, belongs to the fairly large class of works which Schürer designates "Jewish propaganda under a heathen mask." In Prof. Andrews' words, "it is not too much to say that the writer's one object is to demonstrate the supremacy of the Jewish people—the Jewish priesthood, the Jewish law, the Jewish philosophy and the Jewish Bible."

On the other hand, criticism of the work has in recent years entered on a new phase, and in one direction has to some extent rehabilitated our author. As long ago as 1870, when the importance of the Egyptian papyri was not fully recognized and the recovered documents were few, Prof. Lumbroso wrote,[1] perhaps with some slight exaggeration, "There is not a court title, an institution,

[1] *Recherches sur l'économie politique de l'Égypte sous les Lagides*, p. xiii.

a law, a magistracy, an office, a technical term, a formula, a remarkable turn of language in this letter, there is no piece of evidence of Aristeas concerning the civil history of the epoch, which is not found registered in the papyri or the inscriptions and confirmed by them." This statement is, on the whole, borne out by the much larger collections of papyri now available, with this important reservation that the titles, formulas, etc., appear, in some instances at least, to be those of the later, not the earlier, Ptolemaic age. Thus, the phrase "if it be *thy* good pleasure" (§ 32), where the pronoun is unrepresented in the Greek, is not found in the papyri before 163 B.C., nor the use of the plural in the phrase "of the chief of the bodyguards" (§ 40) before 148 B.C. The author, it must be admitted, is thoroughly conversant with the technical and official language of Alexandria and the court, and it is probable that his interesting incidental allusions to Alexandrian life and customs are equally trustworthy: the measures taken to counteract the injury to agriculture, produced by migration from country to town (§§ 109 ff.), the treatment of informers (§ 167; cf. § 25), the reception of foreign embassies (§ 182). In these matters the information which he supplies may be used to supplement, where it is not confirmed by, that furnished by the papyri.

If the writer is at home in Alexandrian matters, what weight may be attached to his description of Palestine (§§ 83–120)? Quaint as may be his ideas on *e.g.* the course of the Jordan (§ 117), his description of Jerusalem itself has the vivid touch of an eyewitness. Surely, we are inclined to say, this man was a spectator of the waving curtain or veil at the entrance of the Temple (§ 86), and was given proof on the spot of the existence of the underground cisterns beneath and around the

Temple area (§§ 89–91), of which we learn from other sources. Sir George Adam Smith, indeed, regards the Letter as "the work, perhaps about 200, of a Jewish writer, well acquainted with the city and the land"; "standing upon the Akra . . . this observer had the bulk of the town before him on the South-West and North-West Hills," and his description (§ 105) is given "with remarkable fidelity to their configuration."[1] The date here suggested (after Schürer) is largely based on the picture presented in this section of the political position of Palestine and its relation to Egypt. The fortress of Jerusalem is still in possession of the Jews. Alexandrians are allowed to enter the country and its capital without molestation, and "the Jewish people and their high priest appear as almost politically independent" (Schürer). This, according to Schürer, presupposes the period before the conquest of Palestine by the Seleucid dynasty in 198 B.C. as the date of writing.

This brings us to the question of **date**, as to which there is a considerable diversity of opinion. The Letter was used by Josephus, and was almost certainly known to Philo (see Appendix, pp. 96 ff.). How much earlier is it? Three dates have hitherto been proposed: (1) about 200 B.C. (Schürer); (2) about 100 B.C., or more precisely between 96 and 63 B.C. and nearer the former date (Wendland); (3) more than a century later, under Tiberius or Caligula (Grätz, Willrich).

The last-named date is certainly too late, and the arguments for bringing the work down to the Imperial age, *e.g.* a supposed reference to the Roman *delatores* (§ 167), are unconvincing. The description of Palestine, even if not the first-hand work of the author, could

[1] *Jerusalem*, i. 390; ii. 440.

hardly have stood in its present form after the Roman occupation of Palestine. Nor would the story have been reproduced by Philo if not composed before A.D. 33.

On the other hand, Schürer's date appears to be rather too early. The sketch of Palestine and the Holy City may have been taken over by our author from an earlier writer, Hecataeus of Abdera, to whom he once (§ 31) expressly refers, and of whom there is reason to think that he made a more extensive use. Schürer's other argument is derived from a passage of Aristobulus, who, addressing a Ptolemy commonly identified with Philometor (182–146 B.C.), repeats the statement that the Pentateuch was translated under Philadelphus at the instance of Demetrius Phalereus (see Appendix (5) p. 95). This, in Schürer's opinion, implies that Aristobulus was acquainted with the Aristeas story. The genuineness of the Aristobulus passage has, however, been questioned by many recent critics. It is hard to believe that a fictitious story, as Schürer admits that of Aristeas to be, could have gained credence within little more than half a century after the period to which it relates.

On the whole, an intermediate date, about 120–80 B.C., appears most probable. As already stated, the formulas, etc., employed are those of the later Ptolemaic age. The later Maccabaean age, or the end of the second century B.C., is suggested by some of the translators' names (*e.g.* Jason). Some of Ptolemy's questions indicate a tottering dynasty (§ 187, etc.). The writer appears to borrow his name from a Jewish historian of the second century B.C., and to wish to pass off the latter's history as his own (§ 6). The prologue to the Greek Ecclesiasticus (after 132 B.C.) ignores the Aristeas story, though too much must not be made of this *argumentum e silentio*. The probable allusion (§§ 310 f.) to attempts which had been made to improve on the work of the translators, with the imprecation upon the offender, points to a growing divergence of text which the writer desired to check; with this should be compared the pointed reference to a difference between the Greek text and the Hebrew in a passage of Exodus (§ 57). Allusions to current criticisms of the Pentateuch (§§ 128, 144) presuppose a familiarity with it on the part of non-Jewish readers, only explicable if the LXX had long been current. All these facts point to a date further removed from the age of Philadelphus than that which Schürer would adopt. On the other hand, certain details in the Greek style and orthography seem to preclude a date much later than 100 B.C.

We have, then, to deal with a work which in some respects is obviously fictitious, and in others appears deserving of respect. Behind the romantic and apologetic framework there lies, no doubt, an element of truth. The story appears to be based, in part at least, on ancient popular tradition. Philo tells us (see Appendix, p. 100) that in his day the translation was celebrated by an annual festival, attended by Jews and others, and held on the beach of the island of Pharos.[1] It is improbable that an artificial production like the Aristeas Letter should have occasioned such an anniversary. On the contrary, this piece of evidence suggests the existence of an independent tradition, and that one object of our Letter may have been to supply a demand for a con-

[1] Conversely, the Palestinian Jews observed as a fast day the 8th Tebeth (December-January), on which "the Torah was written in Greek in the days of King Tolmai, and darkness came upon the world for three days" (Appendix (1), p. 89).

nected account of the events commemorated at the festival.

We are left with the difficult task of attempting to disentangle truth from fiction in the main narrative. The various questions raised are fully discussed by Dr. Swete (*Introd. to O. T.*, chap. i). The following statements in the Letter appear deserving of credit. (1) The Pentateuch forms a distinct *corpus* within the Greek Bible; it was translated first and, in view of the homogeneity of its style, as a whole. (2) The translation was produced at Alexandria, as is conclusively proved by the Egyptian influence on its language, to which the new found papyri furnish the closest parallel. (3) The Greek Pentateuch goes back at least as far as the middle of the third century B.C. (The Greek Genesis was towards the end of that century used by the Hellenist Demetrius.) The style is akin to that of the earlier papyri, and reflects the period of the dawn of the *Κοινή* when certain forms were in use which had already become obsolete in New Testament times. (4) It is not unlikely that the task was undertaken by a company of translators, though the traditional number (70 or 72) is certainly legendary. A parallel may be found in a group of prophetical books (Jeremiah, Ezekiel, Minor Prophets), where indications have been traced in the Greek of collaboration and a division of labour between members of a later company. (5) The Hebrew rolls were not improbably imported from Palestine. (6) Possibly Philadelphus, the patron of literature, with his known tastes and his "syncretistic temperament" (Swete) may have countenanced the work.

On the other hand, the assertion that it owed its inception wholly to him and his librarian is incredible. It is known that Demetrius did not fill the office of librarian under that monarch. If he played any part in the work it must have been in the reign of the predecessor of Philadelphus, Ptolemy I (Soter), and Dr. Swete is inclined to believe that the project may have been discussed by him with the royal founder of the Alexandrian library, "and that the work was really due to his suggestion, though his words did not bear fruit until after his death" (*Introd.*, p. 19). There may even be an element of truth in the tradition of an older and less careful translation prior to the time of Philadelphus (cf. Arist. §§ 30, 314). But the existing version is written in the vernacular, not in a literary style suitable to a work produced under royal patronage.

Again, the story of the importation of Palestinian translators is doubtless fictitious. Dr. Swete acutely observes that Aristeas, in relating that the translation was read to and welcomed by the Jewish community before being presented to the king (§§ 308 ff.), unconsciously reveals its true origin. It was produced, we may be sure, to meet their own needs by the large Greek-speaking Jewish colony at Alexandria. Lectionary requirements and a demand that the Law should be read in the synagogues in a tongue "understanded of the people" were, we have reason to conjecture, the originating impulse.

Later Accretions to the Legend[1]

From being the Bible of the Jewish Dispersion the Greek Old Testament became the Bible of the early Church. The traditional story of its birth thus fitly finds a place in a series of documents illustrative of Christian origins. The Church Fathers accepted this story without suspicion and amplified it. Beside these later fabrications the older narrative appears comparatively rational. The translators, it was now asserted, worked independ-

[1] See the Appendix.

ently in separate cells and produced identical versions, Ptolemy proposing this test of their trustworthiness (contrast Arist. § 302, "arriving at an agreement on each point by comparing each other's work"). So say, *e.g.*, Irenaeus, Clement of Alexandria and the authors of the *Chronicon Paschale* and the *Cohortatio ad Graecos* (ps. Justin). The last writer asserts that he had seen the cells and heard the tradition on the spot. According to a modified form of the legend, the translators worked in pairs, in thirty-six cells; so Epiphanius and later writers. Epiphanius enters into great detail. The translators were, he says, locked up in skylighted cells in pairs, with attendants and shorthand writers; each pair was entrusted with one book, the books were then circulated and thirty-six identical versions of the whole Bible, canonical and apocryphal books, were produced; Ptolemy wrote two letters, one asking for the original Scriptures, the second for translators. The story of the two embassies appears already in the second century in Justin's *Apology*; the extension of the translators' work to the Prophets or the whole Bible recurs in the two Cyrils and in Chrysostom. Lastly, the miraculous agreement of the translators proved them to be no less inspired than the original authors; so Irenaeus and others, Philo having already led the way.

It is needless to dwell on these later inventions, the outcome, it seems, of a steadily growing oral tradition at Alexandria; Jerome justly held them up to ridicule, contrasting them with the older and more sober narrative. But a word may be said on a few points. (1) Cave-dwellings in the island of Pharos may well account for the legend of the cells. (2) An ingenious explanation of the origin of the legend of the miraculous consensus of the seventy (or seventy-two) translators has been found (Hastings' *Dictionary of the Bible*, iv. 439 a) in a passage in Exodus xxiv (LXX) to which Epiphanius expressly refers. We there read of seventy elders of Israel who, with Aaron, Nadab and Abihu, form a link between Moses and the people. They do not follow Moses to the top of the mount; they ascend but a little way and are bidden to worship from afar. According to the Greek text, "they saw the place where the God of Israel stood . . . and of the elect of Israel not one perished" (*v.* 11), *i.e.* they were privileged to escape the usual death-penalty for a vision of the Deity. But the verb used for "perish" (*diaphônein*) was uncommon in this sense; "not one disagreed" would be the more obvious meaning. Hence, it may be, arose both the number seventy (or seventy-two) and the legend of the supernatural agreement of the translators, the latter-day intermediaries between Moses and Israel of the Dispersion. When the translations were recited, "no difference was discoverable," writes Epiphanius, using the kindred word *diaphônia*. (3) An element of truth perhaps underlies one item in Epiphanius' generally incredible account, viz. the working of the translators in pairs. The Greek translations of Jeremiah, Ezekiel and the Minor Prophets, judged by their style, form a group and were probably produced *en bloc* by a company of translators. The translations of Jeremiah and Ezekiel fall into two nearly equal parts, a change of translators occurring in the middle of each book, while in other parts of the LXX a variety of practice in certain orthographical details indicates a similar division for clerical purposes. There was, it seems, a primitive custom of transcribing each book on two separate rolls, and in two books at least the practice goes right back to the time when the translation was made.

Bibliography

The most recent editions of the Greek text are those of P. Wendland (Leipzig, 1900, in the Teubner series of classical texts; especially valuable for its Appendix, containing the evidence of Jewish and Patristic writers on the origin of the Greek version, and its full Index of words) and H. St. J. Thackeray, printed as an Appendix to Dr. Swete's *Introduction to the Old Testament in Greek* (Cambridge, 1900, etc.).

An English translation, with introduction and commentary, by Prof. H. T. Andrews, is included in vol. ii of Charles' *Apocrypha and Pseudepigrapha of the Old Testament* (Oxford, 1913); a German version by P. Wendland in vol. ii of Kautzsch's *Apokryphen and Pseudepigraphen des Alten Testaments* (Tübingen, 1900). An English version by the present translator, which appeared first in the *Jewish Quarterly Review* (April 1903) and then as a separate reprint (Macmillan, 1904), is superseded by the present work, except for some notes for which room could not here be found.

An incomplete critical edition with Latin commentary on §§ 1–51, by L. Mendelssohn appeared in 1897. Of critical studies special mention may be made of Swete's *Introduction*, part i, chap. i, and an essay by I. Abrahams in the *Jewish Quarterly Review* for January 1902; an article by P. Wendland is contributed to the *Jewish Encyclopaedia*. For further literature reference may be made to Schürer's *History of the Jewish People*, div. ii, vol. iii, 310 (1897).

The present translation is made from the text in Dr. Swete's *Introduction*, Wendland's edition being consulted throughout. With the kind permission of the former editors (Mr. C. G. Montefiore and Mr. I. Abrahams) and publishers (Messrs. Macmillan) of the *Jewish Quarterly Review*, it is based on the translation which appeared in that journal; but the whole has been carefully revised, with much assistance in particular from the recent version by Prof. Andrews. The translator has also to acknowledge the permission kindly granted by the publishers of *The International Standard Bible Encyclopædia* (Howard-Severance Company, Chicago, 1915) to make use of his article, "Septuagint," contained therein. The sections into which the text is divided are those of Wendland; these are introduced into the later editions of the Cambridge text.

The Appendix contains a selection of the principal passages in Jewish and Christian writings relating to the origin of the version of the Seventy. These are, it is believed, here collected for the first time in an English dress. For the Rabbinic passages, which were not included in Wendland's *Testimonia*, the translator has to acknowledge the kind assistance of one of the Editors of this series, Canon Box.

As regards the use of *italics*, the principle of the Revisers of the Old Testament has in general been followed, viz. "where any doubt existed as to the exact rendering . . ., all words which have been added in order to give completeness to the English expression are printed in italic type, so that the reader by omitting them may be able to see how far their insertion is justified by the words of the original."

THE LETTER OF ARISTEAS

(I) INTRODUCTORY ADDRESS TO PHILOCRATES

As the story of our deputation to Eleazar, the high 1
priest of the Jews, is worth the telling, and because thou, Philocrates, hast set thy heart, as thou art constantly reminding me, on learning the motives and purpose of our mission, I have endeavoured to give thee a clear account of the matter. I know that love of learning of thine;
and it is indeed man's highest task "ever to make 2
addition to his store of learning and acquirements,"[1] either by the study of history or by actual experience of affairs. The soul is thus built up in purity, by taking up into itself what is best, and with piety, supreme above all, as its aim, is assisted in its pursuit by an unerring guide.

It was my[2] devotion to the careful study of religion 3
which led me[2] to offer my[2] services for the embassy to the man I have mentioned, who, owing to his virtuous character and exalted position, is held in high honour both by his countrymen and by the rest of the world, and is in possession of *documents of* the greatest service to his nation, whether at home or abroad, for the translation of the divine law, because it exists in their country written
on parchment in Hebrew characters. This *embassy* then 4

[1] These words form an iambic line in the Greek, and are probably a quotation from a lost tragedy. [2] Lit. "our," "us," "our."

I[1] undertook with enthusiasm, after finding an opportunity
of *approaching* the king on the subject of the men who
were removed to Egypt from Judaea by the king's father,
when first he took over the city[2] and the government
of Egypt. This story also it is worth while my telling
5 thee. For I am persuaded that thou above all men,
with thy leanings towards the holiness and the senti-
ments of the men who live in accordance with the
holy law, wilt gladly listen to the story about them
which I[1] purpose to narrate, having but recently come
over from the island[3] to us and being anxious to
6 hear whatever makes for the soul's edification. On a
former occasion, too, I sent thee a description of matters
in my opinion worthy of record concerning the Jewish
nation, which I[1] obtained from the high priests, the most
7 learned body in that most learned land of Egypt.[4] It is
right to communicate such things to thee with thy eager-
ness to learn what may benefit the mind; very willingly
would I *impart them* to all who are like-minded with thee,
but chiefly to thee; so sincere are thy principles, and not
only does thy character shew thee to be my brother by
birth, but in thy striving after goodness thou art at one
8 with me.[5] For neither the attraction of gold nor any other
of the objects that the vain-glorious hold in honour confers
the same benefit as a cultured training and the pains ex-
pended thereon. But, not to weary you with too long an
introduction, I[1] will resume the thread of the narrative.[6]

[1] Lit. "we." [2] Alexandria.

[3] Probably Cyprus is meant.

[4] Possibly the writer wishes to identify himself with the historian Aristeas, who wrote a work about the Jews, a fragment of which is preserved by Eusebius.

[5] Lit. "with us." Perhaps with a slight transposition of words we should read, "and not only art thou my brother by birth, but also in thy character, which in its striving after goodness is akin to ours,"

[6] Cf. 2 Macc. ii. 32.

(II) ORIGIN OF THE SCHEME AND PRELIMINARY PROCEEDINGS

(*a*) THE PROPOSAL OF THE KING'S LIBRARIAN

Demetrius of Phalerum,[1] as keeper of the king's 9
library, received large grants of public money with a
view to his collecting, if possible, all the books in the
world; and by purchases and transcriptions he to the
best of his ability carried the king's purpose into execution.
Being asked once in my[2] presence, about how many thou- 10
sands of books were already collected, he replied "More
than two hundred thousand,[3] O king; and I will ere long
make diligent search for the remainder, so that a total of
half a million may be reached. I am informed that the
Jews also have certain laws which are deserving of
transcription and a place in thy library." "What is to 11
hinder thee, then," replied the king, "in this task? For
all the necessary means are at thy service." And De-
metrius answered, "Translation is also required. For in
the Jews' land they use a peculiar script (just as Egyptians
have their system[4] of letters) and speak a peculiar
language. It is commonly thought that they use the
Syrian[5] language, but this is an error; it is another
dialect." And when the king had learnt all the facts, he
gave command that a letter should be written to the
high priest of the Jews, in order that the proposal above-
mentioned might be carried into effect.

[1] Demetrius lived from about 345 B.C. to about 283 B.C. The last part of his life was spent at the court of Ptolemy Soter, but he was out of favour with Ptolemy Philadelphus and banished by him. He was never the royal librarian.

[2] Lit. "our."

[3] Gr. "tens of thousands."

[4] Lit. "arrangement."

[5] *i.e.* Aramaic.

(*b*) THE EMANCIPATION OF THE JEWISH SLAVES.

12 And now thought I was the opportunity for introducing
a matter about which I had often made request to Sosibius of Tarentum and Andreas, the heads of the bodyguard, namely, the liberation of the Jews who had been carried away from Judaea by the king's father. For he, after overrunning the whole of Coele-Syria and Phoenicia, assisted by good fortune and his own prowess, transplanted some and made prisoners of others, terrorizing and reducing the whole country to submission. It was on this
occasion that he carried away more than a hundred
13 thousand persons from the Jews' country into Egypt, of
which number he armed about thirty thousand picked men and settled them in the fortresses in the country. (Many Jews had already before this entered the country along with the Persian,[1] and others had at a still earlier time been sent out as auxiliaries to fight in the army of Psammetichus [2] against the king of the Ethiopians; but
these immigrants were not so large a body as those whom
14 Ptolemy, son of Lagus, introduced.) Well, as we said
before, he selected those who were best fitted *for service* by age and physique, and armed them, but the remaining mass, those who were too old or too young for service, and the women as well, he reduced to bondage, not of his own free will, but rather compelled thereto by the soldiers, *who claimed them* in return for the services which they had rendered in action.

Having, therefore, found some pretext for their release,

[1] Cambyses, who conquered Egypt in 525 B.C.

[2] Psammetichus was king of Egypt from about 671 to 617 B.C.; he was the first king of Egypt to employ *Greek* mercenaries in foreign campaigns (Hdt. II. 151 ff.). Others think that Psammis or Psammetichus II, as he is sometimes called, is here intended. He became king of Egypt in 601 B.C., and waged war against Ethiopia (Hdt. II. 159–161).

as already explained, I[1] addressed the king somewhat as
follows: "It would surely be unreasonable, O king, to 15
let our deeds give the lie to our words. For, as the laws
which we are proposing not only to transcribe but also to
translate are binding on all Jews, what justification shall
we find for our mission, whilst large numbers of the race
continue in slavery in thy kingdom? Nay, with a perfect
and bounteous heart release those who are held fast in
miseries, since the same God who gave them their law
directs thy kingdom, as my research has taught me.
For the God who sees and created all things whom 16
they worship is He whom all men worship, and we too,
O king, though we address Him by other names as Zeus
and Dis; and by these names they of old time not in-
appropriately signified that He, through whom all things
receive their life and being, is the Director and Lord of
all.[2] Outdo, then, all men in magnanimity, and set at
liberty those who are held in bondage."

The king kept silence for a while, and I[1] inwardly 17
prayed to God to dispose his mind to a general release.
(For the human race, being God's creation, is swayed
and moved by Him; and therefore I called with many
and divers prayers upon Him that rules the heart, that
he might be constrained to fulfil my desire. For I had 18
a good hope, in bringing forward a proposal concerning
the deliverance of men,[3] that God would cause the fulfil-
ment of my desires; for when men piously think that
they are working for righteousness and the furtherance of
good deeds, it is God Almighty who directs their actions

[1] Lit. "we."

[2] The two accusative forms of Ζεύς, viz. Ζῆνα and Δία, are here derived from ζῆν (to live), and διά (through). This etymology is found in Orphic and other writings; see the Orphic fragment quoted by Blass on Acts xvii. 28.

[3] Cf. § 292. It is unnecessary to read "the men."

and designs.) But the king, raising his head and looking
19 at me with a cheerful countenance, said, "How many thousands[1] dost thou suppose there will be?" And Andreas, who was standing close by, replied, "A little over a hundred thousand." "Of a truth," said he, "it is but a small request which Aristeas makes of us." But Sosibius and some others who were present said, "It is indeed an action worthy of thy magnanimity to offer the release of these men as a thank-offering to the Most High God. For, as thou hast been most highly honoured by the Almighty and exalted above thy forefathers, so is it fitting that thou shouldest make the very highest of
20 thank-offerings." And he, greatly delighted, gave orders that *the redemption money* should be added to the *soldiers'* pay: for every slave *the owner* should receive twenty drachmas: a decree should be published on the subject, and the registers should be drawn up forthwith. So magnificent was his zeal, and thus did God fulfil our whole desire, constraining him to liberate not only those who had entered the country with his father's army, but also any who were there before or had since been introduced into the kingdom.[2] It was pointed out that the donation would exceed four hundred talents.

21 And I think that it will not be without use to have on record here a copy of the decree. For the munificence of the king, who was empowered by God to be the means of deliverance to vast multitudes, will thus be made far clearer and more evident. It ran thus:—

22 "BY THE KING'S DECREE.

"All persons who served in the campaign of our father against the regions of Syria and Phoenicia and in the

[1] Gr. "tens of thousands."

[2] Possibly some words have here fallen out in the MSS.

invasion of the territory of the Jews, and became possessors of Jewish slaves, and have brought these over into the city *of Alexandria* and the country *of Egypt*, or have sold them to others — likewise also if any such were beforetime *in the country* or have since been introduced —the owners shall straightway release them. Compensation shall forthwith be paid for every slave twenty drachmas, to the soldiers with their pay, and to the rest
at the royal bank. We consider that the making of these 23
persons prisoners was contrary to the will of our father and to justice, and that the spoliation of their country and the transportation of the Jews into Egypt were due to military recklessness. The spoil which accrued to the soldiers on the field of battle should have sufficed; to reduce the people to subjection in addition was wholly
inequitable. Forasmuch then as it is our recognized 24
practice to award justice to all men, but chiefly to those who are unreasonably oppressed, and we do always strive to deal fairly with all men in accordance with the dictates of justice and piety, we have decreed that the owners of all Jewish persons who are held in bondage anywhere[1] in any manner within the kingdom, shall on receipt of the prescribed sum release them. No one shall in any way be dilatory in the discharge of these duties, but within three days from the date of publication of this decree they shall hand in their lists to those who are set over this business, and shall also at once produce the
persons. For we are resolved that it is expedient for 25
ourselves and for the realm that this matter be accomplished. Any who will may give information concerning defaulters, on condition that the informer shall become owner of the person if found guilty, but the

[1] Emended text.

property of such persons shall be confiscated to the royal purse."

26 When the decree was submitted to be read over to the king, containing all the rest with the exception of the words, "Also if any such were beforetime *in the country* or have since been introduced," the king himself out of his munificence and magnanimity appended this clause. He also gave orders to assign a grant of the moneys in a lump sum to the paymasters of the forces
27 and the royal bankers. The matter was thus decided and the decree was ratified within seven days. The donation amounted to over six hundred and sixty[1] talents; for many children at the breast were also liberated along with the mothers. When the further question was referred, whether twenty drachmas should be given for these as well, the king ordered that this also should be done. So thoroughly in every detail did he give effect to the decision.

(*c*) THE LIBRARIAN'S MEMORIAL.

28 And when this business was ended, he ordered Demetrius to submit a statement concerning the transcription of the Jewish books. For all business used to be transacted by these kings[2] by means of decrees and with great precaution, and nothing was done in an offhand or casual manner. And therefore have I set down here copies of the memorial and the letters, and the number of the presents sent, and the nature of each, for every one of these excelled in magnificence and technical skill. And the following is a copy of the memorial:—

[1] Josephus writes, "over 460 talents."

[2] The writer here betrays that he lived at a later age than that which he is describing.

"To the great king from Demetrius—In obedience 29
to thy order, O king, that the books which are wanting
to complete the library should be added to the collection, and that those which are defective should be duly
repaired, I have expended great care upon these matters
and now submit a reference to thee. The books of the 30
Jewish law with some few others are wanting. They
are written in Hebrew letters and in the Hebrew tongue,
and have been interpreted[1] somewhat[2] carelessly and
do not represent the original text, according to information supplied by the experts, because they have never
received a king's fostering care. It is necessary that these
books too should in an emended form find a place in 31
thy library, because this code of laws, in that it is divine,
is full of wisdom[3] and faultless. For this reason authors,
poets, and the mass of the historians have abstained from
any mention of the books aforesaid and of the men who
have lived [and are living][4] in accordance with them,
because the views presented in them have a certain
sanctity and holiness, as says Hecataeus of Abdera.[5] If
then it be *thy* good pleasure, O king, a letter shall be 32
written to the high priest at Jerusalem, bidding him send
six elders from each tribe, men of the highest repute
and versed in their country's law, in order that we may
test wherein the more part agree, and so obtaining an

[1] If σεσήμανται is correctly rendered, there appears to be a reference to an earlier Greek translation of the Law than the LXX (cf. § 314). Aristobulus in a well-known passage refers to such a translation (see Appendix, p. 95, Swete, *Introd. to O. T.*, p. 1 f.). Σεσήμανται may, however, merely mean "committed to writing." The explanation of Diels that incorrect vocalization is referred to is ingenious.

[2] Or "very."

[3] Lit. "most" (or "more") "philosophical."

[4] Perhaps a gloss.

[5] A contemporary of Alexander the Great and Ptolemy I and author of a history of Egypt. Cf. §§ 312 ff.

accurate translation may deposit it in a conspicuous place[1] in a manner worthy of the undertaking and of thy
33 gracious will. Fare ever well!"[2] When this memorial had been presented, the king ordered that a letter should be written to Eleazar on these matters, informing him also of the emancipation of the captives. He presented also towards the construction of bowls and vials and a table and cups for libations fifty talents' weight of gold and seventy talents of silver and of precious stones a great number (enjoining the treasurers to leave to the craftsmen the selection of such materials as they might desire), and for sacrifices and other purposes as much as an hundred talents in money.

(*d*) THE LETTERS OF PTOLEMY AND ELEAZAR

34 I[3] will give thee an account of the construction *of the gifts* when I[3] have set out copies of the letters. The tenour of the king's letter was as follows:—

35 "King Ptolemaeus to Eleazar the high priest greeting and health.

"Forasmuch as there are many Jews settled in our realm who were forcibly removed from Jerusalem by the Persians at the time of their power, and others who
36 entered Egypt as captives in the train of our father—of these he enrolled many in the army, giving them higher than the ordinary pay, and in like manner, having proved

[1] *i.e.* in the Alexandrian library (cf. § 38). But the sense is doubtful; possibly we should translate "may make the meaning plain."

[2] Εὐτύχει, as Mahaffy has shown, is the regular formula at the end of an address from a subordinate to his superior, and is therefore correctly used here. A person addressing his subordinate or his equal uses ἔρρωσο (so in the letters that follow, §§ 40, 46).

[3] Lit. "we."

the loyalty of those who were already in the country, he
placed under their charge the fortresses which he built,
that the native Egyptians might[1] be intimidated by
them; and we too since ascending the throne meet all
men, but chiefly thy countrymen, in a very friendly
spirit—we, then, have given liberty to more than a 37
hundred thousand captives, paying their owners the
proper market price, and making good any wrong which
they may have suffered through the passions of the mob.
Our intent in this was to do a pious action and to
dedicate a thank-offering to the Most High God, who has
preserved our kingdom in peace and in the highest
esteem throughout the whole world. Moreover, we
have drafted into the army those who are in the prime
of life, and to such as are fitted to be attached to our
person and deserving of the confidence of court have we
assigned offices of state. Now since we desire to confer 38
a favour not on these only, but on all Jews throughout
the world and on future generations, it is our will that
your Law be translated from the Hebrew tongue in use
among you[2] into Greek, that so these writings also may
find a place in our library with the other royal volumes.
Thou wilt therefore do well and wilt repay our zeal, if 39
thou lookest out six elders from each tribe, men of high
repute, well versed in the Law and able to translate, that
we may discover wherein the more part agree; for the
investigation concerns matters of more than ordinary
import. We think to gain great renown by the fulfil-
ment of this task. We have sent on this business 40
Andreas, of the chief of the bodyguards, and Aristeas,
who hold honoured places in our court, to confer with

[1] So Josephus and Eusebius. The Aristeas MSS insert a negative.
[2] Or "as you call it."

thee. They bring with them dedicatory offerings for the temple, and for sacrifices and other purposes an hundred talents of silver. And shouldest thou also write to us concerning my desires, thou wilt do a favour and a friendly service; and be assured that thy wishes will receive instant fulfilment. Farewell."

41 To this letter Eleazar replied appropriately[1] as follows:—

"Eleazar the High Priest to King Ptolemaeus, his sincere friend, greeting. Do thou fare well and the queen Arsinoe, thy sister, and the children,[2] so will it be
42 well and as we desire; we too are in good health. On receiving thy letter we greatly rejoiced because of thy purpose and noble resolve, and we collected the whole people and read it to them, in order that they might know thy pious reverence for our God. We shewed them also the vials which thou sentest, twenty of gold and thirty of silver, the five bowls, and the table as dedicatory offerings, and the hundred talents of silver for the offering of sacrifices and for such repairs as
43 the temple may require. These gifts were brought by Andreas, one of thy honoured courtiers, and Aristeas, good men and true and of excellent learning, who in all ways worthily reflect thy high principles and righteousness. They have also imparted to us thy message, and have heard from our lips a reply in accordance with thy
44 letter. For in all things which are to thy profit, even though thy request is contrary to our natural impulses,[3] will we do thy bidding; this indeed is a mark of friendship and affection. For thou too hast in divers manners

[1] Or "to the best of his ability." Perhaps "so far as he could write Greek," the writer excusing the use of this language by a Jew of Palestine (Wendland).

[2] Arsinoe II, here referred to, is said to have been childless but to have adopted the children of Arsinoe I.

[3] Lit. "contrary to nature."

done great services to our countrymen which can never
pass out of mind. We therefore straightway offered 45
sacrifices on thy behalf and on behalf of thy sister and
thy children and thy friends,[1] and the whole people
prayed that thy undertakings might ever prosper, and
that Almighty God would preserve thy kingdom in peace
with honour, and that the translation[2] of the holy Law
might be to thy profit and carefully executed. And in 46
the presence of them all we selected six elders from each
tribe, good men and true, whom we are also sending with
a copy of the Law. Thou wilt then do well, righteous
King, to give orders that, so soon as the translation[2] of
the books be accomplished, the men be restored to us
again in safety. Farewell.

THE NAMES OF THE TRANSLATORS

"And their names[3] are, of the first tribe, Joseph, 47
Ezekias,[4] Zacharias, John, Ezekias,[4] Elisha: of the
second, Judas, Simon, Samuel,[5] Adaius,[6] Mattathias,
Eschlemias[7]: of the third, Nehemias, Joseph, Theo-
dosius, Baseas, Ornias, Dakis: of the fourth, Jonathas, 48
Abraius, Elisha, Ananias, Zacharias,[8] Chelkias[8]: of the
fifth, Isaac, Jacob, Jesus, Sabbataius, Simon, Levi: of
the sixth, Judas, Joseph, Simon, Zacharias, Samuel,[5]
Selemias: of the seventh, Sabbataius, Zedekias, Jacob, 49
Isaac, Iesias,[9] Natthaius: of the eighth, Theodosius,

[1] A court title. [2] Or "transcription."

[3] The names, according to Josephus, form a postscript to the letter.

[4] One of these names is probably corrupt.

[5] Text "Somoelus." [6] Either Adaiah (עדיה) or Iddo (עדוא).

[7] Representing שלמיה, which is more correctly represented by Σελεμίας in § 48.

[8] The names Zacharias, Chelkias are derived from the list in the Syriac version of Epiphanius, *De mens. et pond.*, who uses the narrative of Aristeas (see Appendix, p. 111 f.). In the MSS of Aristeas Χαβρίας stands in place of Zacharias and the sixth name in this tribe has disappeared.

[9] Probably = Jesse (Epiphan. אישי).

Jason, Jesus, Theodotus, John, Jonathas: of the
ninth, Theophilus, Abraham, Arsamus, Jason, En-
50 demias, Daniel: of the tenth, Jeremy, Eleazar,
Zacharias, Baneas, Elisha, Dathaius[1]: of the eleventh,
Samuel, Joseph, Judas, Jonathes, Caleb,[2] Dositheus:
of the twelfth, Isaelus, John, Theodosius, Arsamus,
Abietes, Ezekiel: in all seventy-two persons."
51 Such, then, was the reply which Eleazar[3] gave to the
king's letter.

(III) DESCRIPTION OF THE ROYAL PRESENTS

I will now fulfil the promise which I made to describe
the works of art. They were wrought with extraordinary
skill, as the king, in addition to his large grants, also
exercised a constant supervision over the craftsmen, so
that they could not neglect or scamp any part of the
52 work. I will first give thee an account of the table.
Now, the king's intention was to make this piece of work
of gigantic dimensions. However, he caused inquiries
to be made of persons in the locality as to the size of the
previous table[4] which stood in the temple at Jerusalem;
53 and when they reported the dimensions, he inquired
further whether he should make one on a larger scale.
Some of the priests and of the people said that there
was nothing to prevent him. But the king replied that,
though his wish was to make his gift five times as large,
yet he doubted whether such a table might not be
54 useless for the public ministrations. It was not his
desire that his offerings should merely be placed in the
temple; it would afford him far greater satisfaction, if

[1] Or Thaddaeus, as one MS reads.
[2] So Epiphanius. The MSS have Χαβεῦ.
[3] Or "El. and his colleagues." [4] *i. e.* the table of shewbread.

the appropriate services were duly performed by the proper ministers on the structures which he had designed.
He added that the small scale on which the former 55
works were constructed was not due to any lack of gold, but was apparently so planned for some definite reason. For[1] had any injunction been given[1] *for a larger table*, there would have been no lack *of means*; it was not therefore right to surpass or exceed the fit measurements.
At the same time he ordered that the utmost diversity 56
of artistic skill should be employed, for all his conceptions were on a grand scale, and he had a natural gift *of imagination* enabling him to picture the appearance which objects would present.[2] He gave orders too that details as to which there were no instructions in *the Jewish* Scripture should be beautified; wherever written directions were given, the craftsmen were to be guided by these in the measurements.

So they fashioned *the table* "two cubits in length"[3] 57
and "a cubit and a half in height," making the work "of pure gold" and perfectly solid; I mean, the gold was not overlaid upon other material, but the whole was
one massive plate of beaten metal.[4] And they made 58
"a border of an hand-breadth round about," with "rails that revolved"[5] and bore a design of ropes in relief

[1] Emended text.

[2] Or "for designing the appearance of objects." The artistic talent of Philadelphus is attested by the historians of his time.

[3] Perhaps we should insert, with Josephus, "and a cubit in breadth." The following description, obscure in many details, is an elaboration of the description of the table of shewbread in Exod. xxv. 23 (22) ff. (LXX).

[4] Lit. "the plate . . . was itself affixed." The writer follows the LXX, "gold, of pure gold," as against the Heb., "thou shalt overlay it with pure gold."

[5] Meaning doubtful: lit. "twisted mouldings." In Exodus some kind of cable moulding may be intended. In Aristeas the context, with the paraphrase of Josephus, suggests a triangular "rotatory" bar crowning the "border" and turning on pivots at the corners.

59 marvellously wrought on the three sides. For the rails
were triangular in shape, and the work on each side was
fashioned upon the same pattern, so that, whichever way
they were turned, the appearance was the same; and as
the rail rested on the border[1] that side of it which
sloped towards the table was beautifully worked, although
the side which sloped outwards *alone* met the eye of the
60 spectator. And so the edge in which the two sloping
sides met was a sharp one and, whichever way *the rail*
was turned, held the uppermost place, since, as we have
said already, the shape was a triangular one. And precious
stones were inlaid in the rail between the rope-work;
set one kind beside another they were interwoven in an
61 inimitable manner. And they were all perforated and
securely fastened by golden pins. And at the angles
62 the clamps held them firmly in their places. Over
against the border and slanting upwards to meet the
eyes there was an egg-pattern encircling the table, wrought
of precious stones and elaborately worked[2] with a series
of flutings and relief work, packed closely together round
63 the whole table. And beneath the raised work of the
stones which formed the egg-pattern the craftsmen made
a crown of fruits of all kinds; projecting from it were
shewn vine clusters and corn-ears, dates also and apples
and olives and pomegranates and the like. They worked
the stones, which had the colour of each species of the
aforesaid fruits, to resemble those fruits and attached
64 them to the gold all round the sides of the table. And
next to the crown the egg-pattern was worked over again,
and the rest of the fluted and relief work, because the
table was made to be used on either side according to
choice,[3] and with such symmetry that the rails and the

[1] Text doubtful. [2] Text uncertain.
[3] Text slightly emended.

border reappeared on the side nearest the feet. For 65
they made a plate of solid metal, four fingers broad,
extending along[1] the whole breadth of the table, into
which the legs could be inserted, these being provided
with pins and clamps to secure them to the border, in
order that either side of the table might be used according
to choice.[2] Thus the same appearance was presented
whichever side of the work was placed uppermost.[3]

On the top of the table they worked a "meander"[4] 66
in relief, with costly precious stones of divers kinds[5]
standing out in the middle of it, carbuncles and emeralds
and onyx and stones of other sorts which are noted for
their beauty. And next to the meander there was a 67
wonderful design of open net-work,[6] giving a lozenge-
shaped[7] pattern to the centre of the table; and into this
were inlaid crystal and the so-called electron,[8] affording
an inimitable spectacle to the beholders. And the legs[9] 68
they made with lily-shaped capitals, the lilies bending
over beneath the table, while the parts which met the
eye were the upright leaves. The basis of the leg which 69
rested on the ground consisted entirely of carbuncle, a
hand-breadth *high* and of eight fingers' breadth, and in
appearance had the shape of a shoe; upon this rested
the whole weight[10] of the leg. And they represented 70
ivy, intertwined with acanthus, growing out of the stone
and encircling the leg, together with a vine and its clusters
(these being worked in stone), right up to the top. The
pattern of the four legs was the same; all the parts were

[1] Or "under." [2] Text slightly emended.

[3] Meaning uncertain; text emended (τὸ αὐτὸ for τοῦτο) after Josephus.

[4] Or "maze." [5] Text emended.

[6] Lit. "a wonderful cloven web." [7] Or "rhombus-like."

[8] Probably "amber." [9] Lit. "feet," and so throughout.

[10] Lit. "metal plate" (as in § 65).

carefully made and attached and with such consummate skill and craftsmanship as exactly to resemble nature, insomuch that if a breath of air blew upon them the leaves stirred in their places; so closely was every detail
71 modelled upon the reality. The front[1] of the table they made in three pieces, as it were a triptych, the pieces being fitted together by dovetailing which was secured by pegs in the thickness of the structure, while the joinings were rendered invisible and undiscoverable. The thickness of the whole table was no less than half a cubit, so that *the cost of* the whole work amounted to
72 many talents. For, as the king had determined not to add to its size, he expended all the more upon these details,[2] even as much as would have been required for a table on a larger scale; and in accordance with his purpose the whole was completed in a marvellous and memorable style, with inimitable art and transcendent beauty.

73 Of the mixing-bowls two were wrought in gold, and from their bases to half-way up their sides bore a device of scales in relief, with precious stones cunningly set
74 between the scales. Then above this was a meander, a cubit in height, with its surface[3] wrought out of precious stones of divers hues, and displaying not only beauty but the most elaborate skill. Over this was a mosaic of interlacing lozenge-shaped figures extending to the
75 brim and producing the appearance of net-work. In the middle were bosses of precious stones of various kinds, arranged alternately, and not less than four fingers broad, which enhanced the beauty of the spectacle. Round the crown of the brim were worked lilies with their
76 blossoms and intertwining vine-clusters. Such was the

[1] Lit. "mouth."
[2] Text and meaning doubtful.
[3] Text emended.

fashion of the golden bowls, and they contained over two firkins each. The silver bowls had a smooth surface, and formed a veritable mirror, the marvel of them consisting in this very smoothness, which was such that anything brought close to them was reflected more clearly
than in mirrors. But it is impossible to describe the 77
real impression produced by the completed[1] works of art. For when the vessels were finished and were set side by side—that is to say, first a silver bowl, then a golden, then another silver and another golden one—the nature of the sight was quite indescribable, and those who came to view it could not tear themselves from it, so dazzling was the brilliance and so entrancing the
vision. There was variety in the effect of the spectacle. 78
If one looked at the gold work, it was one of enchantment and astonishment, as the mind took in one by one each detail of the execution. And again, when one wished to turn one's eyes to the silver vessels set out before him, all the surrounding objects were reflected, wherever one stood, causing a still greater ecstasy to the beholders. So the artistic skill displayed in the works is quite beyond description.

On the golden vials they engraved vine-wreaths in the 79
centre, and about the rims they entwined in relief work a wreath of ivy and myrtle and olive, in which they set precious stones. And the rest of the relief work they wrought in various patterns, holding it a point of honour to make everything in a manner worthy of the king's
majesty. In a word, neither in the king's treasury nor 80
in any other was there the like of these works for costliness and artistic skill. No little thought was spent upon them by the king, who loved to gain a reputation for the excellence of his designs. For ofttimes 81

[1] Text (lit. "completed beforehand") doubtful.

he would neglect his public business[1] and would carefully supervise the craftsmen, to see that they executed the works in a manner befitting the place to which they were to be sent. And so they were all made in a magnificent style and were worthy of the king who was sending them and of the high priest who was the governor
82 of the place. So lavish was the supply of precious stones (not less than five thousand were used, and they were all of large size), and so first-rate was all the craftsmanship, that the expenditure upon the precious stones and the skilled work amounted to five times the value of the gold.

(IV) DESCRIPTION OF JERUSALEM AND ITS VICINITY

83 I have given thee this description of the presents because I considered it to be necessary. The next portion *of my letter* contains an account of our journey to Eleazar; but first I will describe the situation of the whole country. When we reached the district, we beheld the city set in the centre of the whole of Judaea upon a mountain which rose to a great height.

(*a*) THE TEMPLE: ENTRANCE, VEIL, ALTAR

84 Upon its crest stood the temple in splendour, with its three enclosing walls, more than seventy cubits high, and of a breadth and length matching the structure of the edifice. The whole was built with a magnificence and
85 prodigality beyond all precedent. It was obvious that no expense had been spared on the great doorway and the fastenings which held it to the door-posts and the
86 stability of the lintel. And the curtain was made very

[1] Or "levee," giving audience to ambassadors, etc.

closely to resemble a door;[1] the fabric was kept in perpetual motion by the draught of wind underneath which caused it to bulge out from bottom to top,[1] and the effect was a beautiful spectacle, from which it was hard to tear oneself away.

The altar was built of a size in keeping with the place 87
and with the sacrifices which were consumed by fire, and the ascent to it was on a like scale. The place was approached by a gradual slope from a proper regard for decency,[2] and the ministering priests were clad in "coats of fine linen"[3] reaching to the ankles.

(*b*) THE TEMPLE WATER SUPPLY

The Temple[4] looks towards the east, and its back is 88
turned westwards. The whole floor is paved with stones and slopes down to the appropriate places, so as to admit of its being flushed with water to wash away the blood from the sacrifices; for many thousand beasts are offered
on the feast days. The water-supply is inexhaustible. 89
An abundant natural spring bubbles up within the temple area. There are, moreover, wonderful underground reservoirs passing description, at a distance, as they pointed out to me, of five furlongs all round the site of the temple, each with innumerable pipes, so that the various channels
converge. *It was explained*, too, how all these cisterns had 90
their bases and sides overlaid with lead, and over them is laid a great mass of plaster, so that everything is made secure; and how there are numerous outlets at the base *of the altar*, which are invisible to all except the actual ministrants, so that all the vast accumulation of sacrificial

[1] Text and meaning not quite certain.
[2] Cf. Exod. xx. 26.
[3] Exod. xxxvi. 35 LXX (xxxix. 27 M. T.).
[4] Lit. "house."

91 blood is swept away in the twinkling of an eye. Such
is my belief as to the nature of the reservoirs, and I
will explain how it was confirmed. They led me more
than four furlongs out of the city, and at a certain place
bade me stoop down and listen to the rushing noise of
the meeting of the waters; thus was the magnitude of
the receptacles made evident to me, as I have described
them.

(*c*) THE PRIESTS AND THE PUBLIC SERVICES

92 The priests' ministration in its exhibition of physical
strength and in its orderly and silent performance could
in no way be surpassed. For they all of their own free
will undergo labours requiring much endurance, and
each has his appointed task. Their service is without
intermission, some *providing* the wood, others oil, others
fine wheat flour, others the spices; while others again
bring the pieces of flesh for the burnt-offering, displaying
93 extraordinary strength. For they grip with both hands
the legs of the calves, most of which weigh over two
talents, and then with both hands and with wonderful
dexterity fling the beast to a considerable height, and
never fail to plant it on the altar. The portions of the
sheep and goats are, likewise, remarkable for their weight
and fat. For those whose duty it is always select such
beasts as are without blemish and of exceeding fatness,
and then the *service* already described is performed.
94 There is a place set apart for them to rest, where those
who are relieved from duty take their seats. And there-
upon, some of those who have had an interval of relaxa-
tion rise up willingly, without any order for their
95 ministration being given. The deepest silence prevails,
so that one would suppose that there was not a single
person in the place, although the ministers in attendance

number some seven hundred, not to mention the large multitude of those who bring their sacrifices to be offered; everything is performed with reverence and in a manner worthy of the divine majesty.[1]

(*d*) THE HIGH PRIEST'S VESTMENTS

And when we beheld Eleazar in the course of his 96
ministration, and his apparel, and the lustre lent by the wearing of the "coat"[2] wherewith he is clad and the precious stones about his person, we were struck with a great amazement. For there are "bells of gold" around *the border of* his "long robe," giving out a peculiar musical sound, and on either side of these are "pomegranates" embroidered in gay colours of a marvellous
hue. He was girt with a rich and magnificent "girdle,"[3] 97
woven in the fairest colours. And on his breast he wears what is called the "oracle,"[4] wherein are set "twelve stones" of divers kinds, fastened with gold, *bearing* the names of the heads of the tribes according to their original order, each of them flashing forth in
indescribable fashion its own natural hue. On his head 98
he has the "tiara," as it is called, and over this the inimitable "turban,"[5] the consecrated diadem, bearing "engraven" upon "a plate of gold" in holy letters the name of God, set between his eyebrows, full of glory. *Such is the raiment of him*[6] who is judged worthy of these
things in the public services. And the general aspect of 99
these things produces awe and discomfiture, insomuch that one thinks that one has passed into another sphere outside the world; indeed, I confidently affirm that any

[1] Lit. "great divinity."
[2] Exod. xxviii. 4, 31–35.
[3] *Ibid.* 39.
[4] *Ibid.* 15–21; xxxix. 8 ff.
[5] Or "mitre." Exod. xxviii. 36 ff.; Ecclus. xlv. 12.
[6] Some words appear to have fallen out in the Greek.

man who witnesses the spectacle which I have described will experience an amazement and wonder indescribable, and will be profoundly moved in his mind at the sanctity attaching to every detail.

(*e*) THE CITADEL AND ITS GUARDS

100 To obtain an accurate knowledge of everything, we ascended to the citadel of the city, which lies hard by, and looked around us. It is situated on a very lofty spot and is fortified with several towers, which are constructed right up to the top of great blocks of stone, as a defence, so we are informed, to the precincts of the
101 temple; so that, in case of any attack or revolution or invasion of an enemy, no one might effect an entrance within the ring-walls of the Temple.[1] On the towers of the citadel there are engines for discharging missiles and machines of divers kinds, and the place commands the
102 enclosing walls aforementioned. The towers are guarded, too, by the most trusted men, whose achievements have fully proved their loyalty to their country. These men had orders not to quit the citadel, except on the feast days, and then only in turn, nor did they suffer any one
103 to enter it. Even when any injunction was given by their leader[2] to admit any persons as sightseers, great care was exercised, as was shown in our case. For although we were but two unarmed men, they could hardly be brought to admit us to witness the offering of
104 the sacrifices. And they said that they were pledged by oaths to act thus. For they all had sworn, and had of bounden duty and for conscience' sake fulfilled their bond, that they, although numbering five hundred men,

[1] Lit. "house."

[2] Apparently the high priest is meant (cf. § 122).

would not admit more than five persons at the same time; for the citadel was the one protection of the temple, and its founder had thus securely fortified its tower of defence.

(*f*) THE CITY AND ITS STREETS

The city is of moderate proportions, its circuit being 105
about forty furlongs, to give a rough estimate. In the disposition of its towers and of the thoroughfares which appear, some below, some above, with the cross-streets through them, it has the familiar[1] aspect of a theatre. For the ground is irregular, as the city is built on a
mountain. There are also stair-ways leading to the 106
thoroughfares. For some persons take their way along the higher level, and others underneath,[2] and they keep as far as possible from each other on the road because of those who are undergoing the usual purifications, to prevent them from touching any forbidden thing.

(*g*) SMALL AND LARGE CITIES CONTRASTED

It was not without reason that the original founders 107
built the city of convenient proportions, but from a wise insight. For as the country is extensive and fair, and some parts, namely those in Samaria so called, and those adjoining the country of the Idumaeans, are level plain, while other parts are mountainous,[3] namely those adjoining the country of Judaea, the inhabitants must[3] devote their unremitting attention to agriculture and the care of the soil, in order that these latter districts may

[1] Emended text. See on §§ 105 f. G. A. Smith, *Jerusalem*, ii. 440 f.

[2] The meaning is doubtful.

[3] Restored by conjecture, some words having been lost in the MSS.

also thereby obtain a plentiful supply of crops. In this way cultivation of every sort is carried on and an abundant harvest reaped throughout the whole of the
108 aforesaid land. On the other hand, it has been the fate of all large and consequently prosperous cities to be thickly populated themselves, while they neglect the country, as the thoughts of every one are bent on enjoyment, and all men have a natural propensity to pleasure.
109 And this is what happened to Alexandria, a city which surpasses all others in size and prosperity. The country folk by migrating to the town and making a long stay
110 there brought agriculture to a low ebb. And so the king, to prevent them from making a stay, ordered that their visits should not exceed twenty days; and he likewise gave written injunctions to the officials, that if it were necessary to summon any such persons *to town*,
111 they should decide their cases within five days. And as he considered the matter one of great importance, he appointed judges with their subordinates in every district,[1] that so the farmers and their agents[2] might not, while money-making *in the city*, reduce the granaries of the city, I mean the proceeds of agriculture.

(*h*) THE COUNTRY AND ITS PRODUCE: HARBOURS, RIVERS, MOUNTAIN-RANGES

112 We have been led into this digression by Eleazar's admirable exposition to us of the principles just mentioned. Their industry in agriculture is indeed great. For their country is thickly planted with olive trees and is rich in cereal produce and pulse, in vines also and honey in abundance; fruit trees of other kinds and palms are beyond reckoning with them. There are cattle in

[1] The Egyptian "nome." [2] Meaning doubtful.

abundance of all sorts, and rich pasturage for them.
And so they rightly recognized that the rural districts 113
needed a dense population, and they constructed the
city and the villages in correct proportions. A great 114
mass of spices, precious stones, and gold is brought into
the district by the Arabs. For the country is well
adapted for commerce as well as for cultivation, and the
city is rich in the arts and lacks none of the merchandise
that is brought across the sea. It possesses havens well 115
situated which supply its needs, that at Ascalon, and
Joppa, and Gaza, as well as Ptolemais which was founded
by the King,[1] and holds a central position compared
with these places, not being far distant from any of them.
The country enjoys everything in plenty, being well
watered on every side and securely enclosed. Round 116
it there flows the river called the Jordan which never
runs dry. *The country* originally comprised not less than
sixty million acres (although subsequently the neighbouring peoples encroached upon[2] it), and six hundred
thousand men[3] became possessors of lots of a hundred
acres each. The river, like the Nile, rises about the
time of harvest[4] and irrigates a large part of the land.
Over against the district of the people of Ptolemais[5] it 117
issues into another river and this flows out into the sea.
Other brooks,[6] as they are called, flow down *into the plain* and encompass the parts about Gaza and the

[1] *i. e.* Ptolemy Philadelphus.

[2] The text is doubtful. According to another reading we might translate "(when) the neighbouring peoples retired" (*i. e.* were gradually driven back by the Israelites).

[3] Cf. Exod. xii. 37, xxxix. 3, LXX; Numb. xi. 21. "A hundred-acre man" occurs frequently in the Petrie Papyri of the veterans of Ptolemy II, who received lots of land in the Fayyum.

[4] Cf. Joshua iii. 15.

[5] Text, "the country of the Ptolemaeans" (? Egypt).

[6] Or "mountain-torrents."

118 region of Azotus. The country is encircled by natural defences, so that invasion is difficult and impracticable for large numbers, because the passes are narrow, being flanked by steep cliffs and deep ravines, and the whole mountain-range which surrounds the entire country is of a rugged character.

(*i*) THE MINES OF ARABIA

119 We were further told that there were formerly copper and iron mines in the neighbouring mountains of Arabia. But these were stopped at the time of the Persian rule, as the overseers of those days spread a false report that
120 their working was unprofitable and expensive, in order to prevent the country from being spoiled for the sake of the mining of the said metals and possibly taken out of their hands as a consequence of the Persian over-lordship, while by the help of this false report they found a pretext for entering the district.[1]

(V) ELEAZAR'S FAREWELL TO THE TRANSLATORS

I have now given thee, dear brother Philocrates, such a summary description of these matters as was necessary. The story of the translation we will tell in the sequel.
121 Well, *Eleazar* selected the men of the best character and the highest culture, such as one would expect from their noble parentage. They were men who had not only acquired proficiency in Jewish literature, but had studied
122 most carefully that of the Greeks as well. They were therefore well qualified to be sent on embassies, and undertook this office whenever occasion required. They possessed

[1] The meaning of this section is obscure.

a great genius for conferences and discussions bearing on the law. They cultivated the due mean, the best of courses,[1] and while they abjured a harsh and uncouth disposition, they were likewise above conceit and the assuming of an air of superiority over others, and in conversation they were ready to listen and to give an appropriate reply to every question. And this bearing they all observed, and it was in such conduct that they most desired to outstrip each other, being all worthy of their
leader and of his virtue. And one might see, in their 123
unwillingness to be torn from him, how they loved Eleazar and he them. For not only did he write to the king on the subject of their safe return, but he also earnestly besought Andreas to work *for the same end*, and urged me[2] too to assist to the best of my[3] power.
And although we promised to give good heed to his 124
wishes, he said that he was deeply distressed, for he knew how the king in his love of goodness considered it the greatest of privileges, wherever he heard of any one who surpassed his fellows in culture and wisdom, to
summon him to his court. Indeed, I have heard of a 125
fine saying of his, that by having about his person just and prudent men he would possess the greatest protection for his kingdom, since friends unreservedly offer advice for one's best interests. And these qualities were assuredly possessed by the men whom Eleazar was now
sending. And he kept asseverating on oath that he 126
would not let the men go, if it were merely some private interest of his own which impelled him so to do, but it was only for the common benefit to all his countrymen
that he was sending them. For, *he added*, a good life 127

[1] With this praise of "the mean" cf. §§ 223 and 256. The writer clearly favours the Peripatetic school.

[2] Lit. "us."

[3] Lit. "our."

consisted in the observance of the laws, and this end was attained much more by oral communication than by reading. From these and similar observations it was clear what were his feelings towards them.

(VI) ELEAZAR'S APOLOGY FOR THE JEWISH LAW

128 It is worth while briefly to mention the explanations given by him in reply to our inquiries. For I suppose that most men feel some curiosity about the regulations in the law[1] concerning meats and drinks and the animals
129 which are considered unclean. Well, when we inquired why, although there was but a single creation, some things are considered unclean for food, and some even to the touch (for the law is scrupulous in most things, but in these matters it is excessively[2] scrupulous), he began his reply as follows:—
130 "Thou seest," he said, "what an influence is exercised by intercourse and association. By associating with evil persons men become perverted and are rendered miserable all their life long, whereas, if they consort with the wise and prudent, they pass from ignorance and amend
131 their lives. Our lawgiver, then, in the first place enjoined[3] piety and righteousness, and expounded them point by point, not merely by prohibitions but also by positive commands, making plain the harmful effects *of disobedience* and the visitations sent by God upon the
132 guilty. In the very first place of all he taught that God is one, and that His power is made manifest through all things, every place being filled with His sovereignty, and

[1] Cf. Lev. xi.; Deut. xiv. 3–20. Compare the treatment of the same subject in the Epistle of Barnabas, § 10.
[2] Text doubtful; perhaps "doubly scrupulous."
[3] Or "laid down the principles of."

that none of the things done in secret by men on earth is hidden from Him, but all that a man does and all
things that are yet to be are manifest in His sight. When 133
he had carefully elaborated these points and made them plain, he shewed that even if a man should but think of acting basely, let alone the doing of the wrong, he could not be hid; thus throughout the whole of the law he displayed the power of God.

"Beginning with these premises he went on to shew 134
that all other men except our nation consider that there are many gods, although they are themselves far more
powerful than those whom they vainly reverence. For 135
they make effigies of stone and wood,[1] and assert that they are images of those who discovered something useful for their life, and these they worship, although their
senselessness is obvious.[2] For that any one should thus 136
become a god in virtue of his invention is altogether foolish; for *the inventors* but took certain created things and put them together and shewed that they possessed a further use, but they did not create the
substances themselves; therefore it is idle and vain to 137
deify men like themselves. Moreover, there are still at the present day many men more inventive and more learned than the men of yore, and yet they would never think of worshipping them. And the framers and authors of these fables consider that they are the wisest of the
Greeks. What further need is there to speak of other 138
infatuated people, Egyptians and the like, who have put their trust in wild beasts and most of the creeping things and vermin, and worship these, and offer sacrifice to these, whether alive or dead?

[1] The treatment of idol-worship and its origin should be compared with Wisdom xiii.–xv.

[2] Or "although it is obvious that they (the images) are without feeling."

139 "When, therefore, the law-giver, who was endowed by God to understand all things, had in his wisdom surveyed each detail, he fenced us about with impregnable palisades and walls of iron, to the intent that we should in no way have dealings with any of the other nations, pure in body and mind, released from vain ideas, reverenc-
140 ing the one Almighty God above the entire creation. For this reason the priests who lead [1] the Egyptians and have closely investigated many things and been conversant with the world,[2] call us "men of God," a designation which does not belong to the rest of mankind, but to him only who reverences the true God. The rest are
141 men of meat and drink and raiment,[3] for their whole nature finds solace in these things. But with our countrymen these things are counted of nothing worth, but their reflections throughout their whole life concern
142 the sovereignty of God. So then, lest we should become perverted by sharing the pollutions of others or consorting with base persons, he hedged us round on all sides with laws of purification in matters of meat and drink
143 and handling and hearing and seeing. For, speaking generally, all things to the natural reason are alike, being all governed by the self-same power, and *yet* in every detail there is a profound reason why we abstain from the use of some things and share in the use of others. For the sake of illustration I will run over one or two points and give thee an explanation.

144 "Do not fall in with the rejected [4] view that it was out of regard for mice and weasels [5] or such creatures

[1] Or "the leading priests of the E. who have," etc.

[2] Lit. "affairs." According to a conjectural reading "(our) literature"; cf. Deut. xxxiii. 1, etc.

[3] Lit. "shelter."

[4] Lit. "fallen down": perhaps "degraded" (Andrews).

[5] Lev. xi. 29. Cf. 1 Cor. ix. 9.

that Moses drew up these laws with such exceeding care. No, all these ordinances have been solemnly made for righteousness' sake, to promote holy meditation
and the perfecting of character. For all the winged 145
creatures, of which we partake, are tame and distinguished by cleanly habits, feeding on wheat and pulse, such as pigeons, turtle-doves, locusts,[1] partridges, geese
too and all the like. But as touching the forbidden 146
winged creatures, thou wilt find that they are wild and carnivorous and use the strength which they possess to oppress the remainder of their kind and get their food by cruelly preying on the aforesaid tame creatures; and not on these only, but they also carry off lambs and
kids, and do violence to dead men and living. By 147
these creatures, then, which he called unclean,[2] the lawgiver gave a sign that those for whom the laws were ordained must practise righteousness in their hearts and oppress no one, trusting in their own strength, nor rob one of anything, but must direct their lives by righteous motives, even as the tame birds above mentioned consume the pulse that grows on the earth and do not tyrannize to the destruction of their kin.

"By such symbols, then, the lawgiver has taught the 148
understanding to note that they must be just and do nothing by violence, nor oppress others in reliance on
their own strength. For whereas it is not meet even to 149
touch the aforesaid creatures by reason of their several natures, what strict precautions must we not take to prevent
the character from degenerating to a like condition? He 150
has, then, set forth all these rules as to what is permitted us in the case of these and the other creatures by way of allegory. For the parting of the hoof and the dividing

[1] Lev. xi. 22. Another reading names a species of moor-fowl.
[2] Deut. xiv. 19.

of the claws[1] symbolize discrimination in our every
151 action with a view to what is right; for the strength of the whole body and its activity are dependent upon the arms[2] and legs. He constrains us, then, to do everything with discrimination and with a view to righteousness; such is the signification of these symbols.[3] He
152 further *signifies* that we are distinct from all men. For most other men defile themselves by promiscuous unions, working great unrighteousness, and whole countries and cities pride themselves on these vices. For not only do they have intercourse with males, but they even defile mothers and daughters.[4] But we have been kept apart from these things.

153 "Again, *the lawgiver* has characterized the possessor of the aforesaid quality of discrimination[5] as possessing also the gift of memory. For 'all things which part the hoof and chew the cud'[6] to thoughtful minds clearly
154 represent memory. For the chewing of the cud[7] is nothing else but a calling to mind of life and existence;
155 for he considers[8] that life exists by taking food. And therefore he gives exhortation by the scripture also where he says thus, 'Thou shalt well remember the Lord who wrought in thee the great and wonderful things.'[9] For, when clearly perceived, they do appear 'great and glorious,' in the first place the construction of the body, and the means for digesting the food, and the distinction

[1] Lev. xi. 3 ff.; Deut. xiv. 6 ff.

[2] Lit. "shoulders."

[3] Text doubtful.

[4] The Egyptian custom of marriage with a sister is passed over without remark.

[5] Or "separation."

[6] Lev. xi. 3.

[7] Cf. Ep. of Barnabas 10, 11; Philo, *De Spec. Leg.* iv. 5; Theodoret, *Quaest.* in Lev. xi. 189.

[8] Or (reading νομίζεται) "life is wont to exist."

[9] A combination of Deut. vii. 18 and x. 21 LXX, the words "in thee" in the latter verse being here referred to the human anatomy, "in thy body."

between the several members; but much more do the 156
orderly arrangement of the senses, the operation and
invisible movement of the mind, and its rapidity in
suiting its action to each several occasion and its dis-
covery of the arts bear the marks of an infinite wisdom.[1]
And therefore he exhorts us to bear in mind, how that 157
the aforesaid things are[2] both created and[2] preserved
by the power of God. For he has appointed every time
and place for the continual remembrance of God, the
Ruler and Preserver. For instance, in the matter of 158
meats and drinks he bids us first to offer a part as a
sacrifice, and not till then to partake of food. In our
clothing, too, he has given us a symbol of remembrance.
Likewise also he has commanded us to set the oracles
'upon our gates and doors,'[3] that God may be had in
remembrance; and he expressly orders that the 'sign' 159
be 'bound round upon the hands,'[4] clearly indicating
that every action must be righteously performed with a
remembrance of our creation, and above all with a fear
of God. And he bids men 'when lying down and 160
when rising up'[5] to meditate on the things which God
has created, not in speech only, but reviewing also in
thought the change and the impression which passes
over them when they fall asleep, and the manner of their
waking, how divine, as it were, and incomprehensible is
the interchange of these states.[6]

"Thou hast now been shewn the exceeding wisdom 161
of the saying[7] concerning discrimination and memory,
according to our exposition of the parting of the hoof and
the chewing of the cud. For the laws have not been
made at random and capriciously, but with a view to

[1] Lit. "contain an infinite manner."

[2] Meaning doubtful: lit. "are preserved . . . with (?) creation."

[3] Deut. vi. 9.

[4] Ibid. 8.

[5] Ibid. 7.

[6] Cf. §§ 213–216 and 3 Macc. v. 11.

[7] Text doubtful.

162 truth and to point the way to right reason. For by his
detailed injunctions concerning meats and drinks and
touch he bids us do and hear nothing heedlessly, nor
to resort to injustice by a misuse of the dominating power
163 of speech.[1] In the case of the wild animals, too, the
same principle may be discovered. For the habits of
'weasel and mouse'[2] and of all the like animals enumer-
164 ated are injurious. Mice mar and injure everything not
only for their own food, but in such a way that anything
which they have begun to injure becomes utterly useless
165 for man. And the weasel tribe is peculiar, for beside
the aforenamed habit it has a characteristic which defiles
it; it conceives through its ears and gives birth through
166 its mouth.[3] And therefore the like habit of man is un-
clean; that is to say, whenever they have embodied in
speech the things which they have received through the
ear and involved others in ills, they are guilty of gross
uncleanness and are themselves utterly tainted with the
pollution of their impiety. And your king, as we are
informed, rightly puts such men to death."

167 And I said, "I suppose that thou speakest of the
informers; indeed he constantly exposes them to tortures
and painful deaths."

"Yes," he replied, "I speak of them. For to watch for
168 men's destruction is an unholy practice. And our Law
forbids us to injure any whether by word or deed.

"In my brief summary of these matters I have shewn thee how every regulation has been made with a view to righteousness, and nothing has been set down in the Scripture heedlessly or in a mythical sense,[4] but its purpose is that throughout our whole life we may in our

[1] Or "the power of reason."

[2] Lev. xi. 29.

[3] Cf. Ep. Barn. x. 8.

[4] Lit. "fabulously." Another reading might mean "capriciously."

actions exercise righteousness towards all men, remembering the sovereignty of God. So then all that is 169
said concerning meats and the unclean creeping things and wild animals relates to righteousness and righteous dealings between man and man."

To my mind, then, he appeared[1] to make an excellent 170
defence in every particular. He added, moreover, with regard to the calves and rams and he-goats that are offered, that men must take these from the herds and flocks and sacrifice tame animals, and nothing that is wild, that so the offerers of the sacrifices, bearing in mind the symbolic meaning of the legislator, may have no arrogant thoughts upon their conscience. For he that presents the sacrifice makes an offering of his own
soul and all its affections. I think that his discourse on 171
these matters was worth repeating; and therefore have I been led on, knowing thy love of learning, dear Philocrates, to explain to thee the sanctity and natural[2] meaning of the Law.

(VII) RECEPTION OF THE TRANSLATORS AT ALEXANDRIA

So Eleazar, when he had offered sacrifice and selected 172
the men and made ready many gifts for the king, sent us
on our way in great security. And when we reached 173
Alexandria, the king was informed of our arrival. On our admission to the court, Andreas and I gave friendly greetings to the king and delivered the letter from
Eleazar. The king was so anxious to meet the delegates 174
that he gave orders to dismiss all the other officials and
to summon the men. This proceeding excited universal 175

[1] Text emended; the MSS have "he thought."
[2] Or "inward": the exact sense is uncertain.

surprise, because the custom is that those who come on official business gain access to the king's presence on the fifth day, while envoys from kings or eminent cities with difficulty secure admission to the court in thirty days. But since he considered the new-comers worthy of higher honour, and rightly estimated the eminent position of him who sent them, he dismissed those whom he considered superfluous, and remained walking to and fro,
176 waiting to greet them on their arrival. When they entered with the gifts which had been sent and the (precious)[1] parchments whereon was inscribed the law in gold in the Jewish characters, the material being wonderfully prepared, and the joining of the several leaves being rendered imperceptible, the king, when he saw the men,
177 began to ask concerning the books. And when they had taken the rolls out of their coverings and unrolled the leaves, the king, after pausing for a long while and making obeisance some seven times, said, "I thank you, friends, and him that sent you still more, but most of all
178 do I thank God, Whose oracles these are." And when all with one accord and with one voice, both the new-comers and the others who were present, exclaimed, "Well *spoken*,[2] O king," he was moved to tears out of the fulness of his joy. For the strain upon the high-strung soul and the overwhelming *sense* of honour where
179 our achievements are successful constrain to tears. He bade them put the rolls back in their places, and then at length did he greet the men and say, "It was right, O God-fearing men, first to pay homage to those treasures, for the sake of which I sent for you, and thereafter to extend the right hand to you; for that reason have I

[1] The word is absent from Josephus' paraphrase and should perhaps be omitted.

[2] Or "Well *be it*," "God save the king."

done this first. I regard this day of your arrival as a 180
great day, and from year to year shall it be held in honour all our long life. Moreover, it happens to be the anniversary of our naval victory over Antigonus.[1] Therefore also it shall be my pleasure to sup with you
to-day. All things," he added, "shall be duly prepared 181
for you in accordance with your *national* customs, and for me with you." And when they had expressed their gratitude, he ordered that the best quarters near the citadel should be assigned to them, and the banquet made ready.

(VIII) THE BANQUET IN HONOUR OF THE TRANSLATORS

So Nicanor, the lord high steward,[2] summoned Doro- 182
theus, who had the charge of guests from this nation, and ordered him to make preparation for everything. For such was the arrangement decreed by the king, and it may still be seen to this day. To every state which has its special usages in matters of drink and meat and in its mode of reclining was there a corresponding official in charge; and then, whenever any person visited the reigning king, preparations were made in accordance with their customs, in order that there might be no discomfort to mar their enjoyment. This practice was followed in
the case of these envoys. Dorotheus, the patron of 183
visitors from their nation, was scrupulously attentive. He laid out all the stores for the banquet which were in his keeping and were set apart for receptions of such guests. And he placed the couches in two rows, according to the king's instructions; for he had ordered him to

[1] See Introduction, p. ix.
[2] Text emended: MSS "the chief physician."

make half of the men recline at his *right* hand, and the remainder behind his own couch, neglecting no means of showing them honour.

184 When they had taken their places, he bade Dorotheus perform the customary rites of all his visitors from Judaea. So he dispensed with the services of the sacred heralds and ministers of the sacrifices and the others who usually offered the prayers, and requested one of those who had come with us, Elisha,[1] the oldest of the *Jewish* priests, to offer a prayer. And he arose and
185 spoke these memorable words: "May the Almighty God give thee thy fill, O king, of all the good things which He has created, and may He grant to thee and thy wife and thy children and to them that are of one mind with thee continual enjoyment of them while life
186 shall last!" At these words there was a burst of applause with shouting and jubilation lasting for some while; and thereafter they betook themselves to the enjoyment of the banquet which had been prepared. All the attendance at table was undertaken by the staff of Dorotheus, among whom were royal pages and some of those who held places of honour at the king's court.

(IX) THE WISE ANSWERS OF THE TRANSLATORS

187 (1) When, after an interval, an opportunity presented itself, the king asked him who occupied the first place at table (they were arranged according to seniority), how he
188 should preserve his kingdom unimpaired to the last. He paused for a moment and replied, "Thou wilt maintain it most securely thus—by imitating the never-ceasing gentleness of God. For if thou shewest longsuffering

[1] So Josephus. The Aristeas MSS call him Eleazar.

and punishest such as deserve punishment more gently than[1] they deserve, thou wilt turn them from wickedness and lead them to repentance."

(2) The king praised his reply, and asked the next one 189
how he should behave in all his actions.[2] And he replied that if he maintained just dealings with all men, he would act in all things for his best interest,[3] considering that every thought is clear to God. "By taking the fear of God for thy starting-point, thou wilt never be disappointed."

(3) To him too he gave his cordial assent, and asked 190
another how he could keep his friends like-minded with himself. And he said, "If they see thee taking great forethought for the multitudes over whom thou rulest; and this thou wilt do by observing how God does good to the human race, in that He provides them with health and food and all else in due season."[4]

(4) He expressed his approval, and asked the next, 191
how when he held his audiences and sat in judgement, he might obtain a good report even from such as failed in their suits. And he said, "If thou art impartial in speech to all alike and never dealest arrogantly nor
tyrannically with offenders. And this thou wilt do if 192
thou beholdest the ordering of God's ways. The deserving have their petitions fulfilled, while to such as fail to obtain them the harmful nature *of their requests* is made known through dreams or events, and God does not smite them according to their sins nor according to the greatness of His might, but uses forbearance."

(5) After highly commending him, he asked his neigh- 193
bour how he might be invincible in warfare. And he

[1] Text emended: MSS "as they deserve."

[2] Or, inserting one word, "do everything *for the best*" (Wendland).

[3] Text uncertain. Perhaps "if he kept himself just towards all, he would act well upon every occasion."

[4] Cf. § 259; also Ps. cxlv. 15, civ. 27; Acts xiv. 17, xvii. 25.

said, "If he did not put his trust in numbers or forces, but always entreated God to give success to his enterprises, while he himself discharged all his duties in a spirit of justice."

194 (6) He approved his reply, and asked the next one how he might inspire terror into his enemies. And he said, "If while maintaining an abundant supply of arms and forces he recognized that these were powerless to produce any lasting and conclusive result; for God also, by granting reprieves and making but a display of his sovereignty,[1] instils terror into every breast."

195 (7) He praised him, and inquired of the next what would be the highest good for his life. And he replied, "To recognize that God is Lord of the Universe, and that in our noblest achievements it is not we ourselves who successfully accomplish our intentions, but God in his sovereignty brings to fulfilment and guides the actions of us all."

196 (8) He admitted the wisdom of his words, and asked the next one how he could preserve all his possessions unimpaired, and finally transmit them to his descendants in the same condition. And he said, "By continual prayer to God that thou mayest be inspired with good thoughts in thy undertakings, and by warning thy descendants not to be dazzled by fame or wealth, since it is God who bestows these gifts, and it is not on their own account that they have pre-eminence over all."

197 (9) He expressed his agreement with this answer, and inquired of him who followed how he should bear with equanimity whatever befell. And he replied, "By taking thought that all men are fashioned by God to partake of the greatest evils, as well as the greatest blessings, and it is not possible for any human being to

[1] Text slightly emended. Cf. with the section Wisdom xii. 16–18.

have no part in them. But God gives a good courage, and we must beseech Him *for the same*."

The king warmly commended him and said that all 198
their answers had been good. "I will put a question to yet one more," *he added*, "and then I will cease for the present, in order that we may turn our thoughts to the enjoyment *of the feast* and make merry. And in the following six days I will gain further enlightenment from each in turn of those who remain."

(10) Thereupon he asked the man, "What is the true 199
aim of courage?" And he said, "To carry out right counsels in the hour of danger in accordance with one's purpose. But thy counsels, O king, are good and are all fulfilled by God to thy profit."

And when they had all signified their assent with loud 200
applause, the king said to the philosophers, of whom not a few were present, "I think that the virtue of these men is extraordinary and their wisdom profound, seeing that, with such questions propounded to them, they have on the spur of the moment given suitable replies, and have all made God the starting-point of their words."
And Menedemus, the philosopher of Eretria,[1] said, 201
"True, O king; for, since the universe is ruled by providence and these men are right in holding that man is a creature of God, it follows that all power and beauty of speech proceed from God."

The king assented thereto, and speeches ceased, and 202
they gave themselves up to festivity. And when evening drew in, the party broke up.

On the following day the guests again took their 203
places and the banquet proceeded in the same order. When the king thought that the time had come to put

[1] See Introduction, p. ix.

inquiries to his guests, he proceeded to question those who were placed next to the men who had given answers on the previous day.

204 (11) He opened conversation with the eleventh (ten having been questioned on the previous day), and when silence was established, inquired how he could continue
205 to be rich. The man to whom the question was addressed paused for a moment and replied, "If he did nothing unworthy of his rulership, never acted licentiously, never expended money on empty and vain things, but by acts of beneficence drew his subjects to wish him well; for God is the author of good things to all men, and man must needs follow His guidance."

206 (12) The king commended him, and asked of another how he should adhere to the truth. To this he replied, "By recognizing that lying brings great disgrace upon all men, but chiefly upon kings. For as they have power to do what they will, what object have they for falsehood? And thou must further take to heart, O king, that God is a lover of the truth."

207 (13) He gave this reply his hearty approval, and looking upon *another* said, "What is the teaching of wisdom?" And the next one replied, "As thou desirest that evils should not befall thee,[1] but to partake of all that is good, thou shouldst act in this spirit to thy subjects and to offenders, and shouldst very gently admonish such as are virtuous; for God draws all men *to Him* by gentleness."

208 (14) He commended him, and asked of his neighbour how he might be humane. And he said, "By observing after how long a time [2] and through what great sufferings

[1] Cf. the Jewish (negative) form of the golden rule, e.g. in the Didache i. 2.

[2] Or, with a slight emendation, "with what trouble" (Wendland).

the human race comes to maturity, aye and to the birth. Thou must not therefore on slight provocation punish or subject men to injuries, recognizing that human life consists of pains and penalties. Thou wilt then, taking all into consideration, be disposed to mercy; for God also is merciful."

(15) With a word of approval to him he inquired of 209
the next in order, "What is the most essential quality for a ruler?" "To keep oneself incorruptible," he replied; "to be sober for the greater part of one's life, to honour righteousness above all things, and to make friends of men of this character; for God also is a lover of righteousness."

(16) He applauded him, and said to the next, 210
"Wherein does piety consist?" And he said, "In the belief that God is working in and has knowledge of all things at all times, and that no unrighteous deed or evil action of man can escape his eye; for as God is the benefactor of the whole world, so wouldst thou, by imitating him, be void of offence."

(17) He signified his assent, and said to the next, 211
"What is the true aim[1] of kingship?" And he said, "To govern oneself aright, and not to be carried away by wealth and fame into extravagant and unseemly desires . . . if thou wouldst reason aright.[2] For thou hast all things at command which are needful[3]; but God has need of nothing and is gentle withal. Let thy thoughts be such as become a man, and reach not after many things, but such only as suffice for thy kingly office."

(18) He commended him and asked the next one how 212
his deliberations might be for the best. And he replied,

[1] Or "essence," "function." [2] Text apparently defective.
[3] Text emended (Wendland): MSS "as nothing."

"If in everything he continually set justice before him and considered injustice to be equivalent to deprivation of life; for God also always promises the greatest blessings to the just."

213 (19) He praised him, and inquired of the next in order how he might be free from disturbing thoughts in sleep. And he said, "Thy question is hard to answer. For in sleep we cannot bring our true selves into play, but are then at the mercy of sensations in which reason
214 has no part. For we have an impression on our minds that we see the things which pass before us, but we are unreasonable if we think that we are indeed on shipboard and ranging over the sea, or flying through the air and passing to other climes, and doing other such things,
215 which we then suppose to be really taking place.[1] Howbeit, my conclusion, so far as I have reached one, is this. Thou shouldest by every means, O king, take piety as the governing motive of thy words and actions, that so thou mayest have the consciousness, while following the path of virtue, of never doing a favour in defiance of reason nor setting justice aside by an abuse of thy
216 power. For, as a rule, the mind is occupied in sleep with the same things in which its waking hours are spent; but every thought and action which is set towards the noblest ends is directed by God[2] both in waking hours and in sleep. And therefore art thou always encompassed with tranquillity."

217 (20) Him too he extolled, and said to the next one, "As thou art the tenth to answer, when thy reply has been given, we will betake ourselves to the banquet." Then he asked, "How can we avoid doing anything unworthy of

[1] Text emended. According to another emendation, "and yet we do suppose these things to be," etc.

[2] Text emended.

ourselves?" And he said, "Look ever to thy fame and 218
eminence, in order that thy words and thoughts may be
in keeping therewith, knowing that all thy subjects think
and talk about thee. For thou must not appear to be 219
worse than[1] the actors, for they look to the part which
they must assume and suit all their actions thereto; but
thou art not acting a part, but art king indeed, God
having given thee the governorship which thy character
merits."

When the king had graciously applauded loud and 220
long, the guests were urged to take some rest.[2] And
when the turn of these men was ended, they betook
themselves to the next service in the order of the
banquet.

(21) On the following day the same order was 221
observed, and when the king thought that the time
was come to put inquiries to the men, he asked the
first of those who yet remained to be questioned, "What
is the highest form of government?" And he replied, 222
"To be master of oneself and not to be carried away by
one's impulses. For all men's minds have some innate
proclivity; probably most men are inclined to eating 223
and drinking and pleasure, while kings are bent on the
acquisition of territory and great renown.[3] But modera-
tion in all things is good. Take what God gives and
keep it, but desire not what is beyond thy reach."

(22) Pleased with his words, the king asked his 224
neighbour how he might be free from envy. And he,
after a pause, said, "Chiefly by considering how it is
God who apportions to all kings their glory and great

[1] Lit. "least of the actors."

[2] Lit. "they urged the men to sleep." Apparently there has been some dislocation in the text.

[3] Text slightly emended.

wealth, and that no one by his own power[1] is king; for all men desire to partake of this glory, but they cannot, since it is a gift of God."

225 (23) He commended the speaker at some length, and asked the next one how he should despise his foes. And he replied, "If thou hast studiously practised goodwill towards all men and formed friendships, thou needest fear no man. But to be in high favour with all men is the very best of good gifts to receive from God."[1]

226 (24) He commended his words, and bade the next one reply to the question, how he might retain his renown. And he said, "If with lovingkindness and gracious acts thou art liberal and bountiful to others, thou wilt never have lack of renown; but that the aforesaid graces may continue thine, thou must constantly call upon God."

227 (25) He belauded him, and asked another, "With whom[1] should we vie in generosity?" And he replied, "All men think that we should be liberal to those who are well disposed to us, but I am of opinion that a keen and open-handed generosity is due to those who dissent from us, that by these means we may win them over to what is right and to their[2] own interest. But one must entreat God that this end may be attained, since He rules the minds of all men."

228 (26) He assented thereto, and bade the sixth man reply to the inquiry, "To whom should favour[3] be shewn?" And he replied, "To parents at all times, since God has given a very great[4] commandment concerning the honour due to parents.[5] And in the second place He sets the attitude of friend towards friend,

[1] Text slightly emended. [2] Possibly "our."
[3] Or "gratitude."
[4] Or "(the) greatest"; cf. Jos. *c. Ap.* II. 27, and, for Rabbinical parallels, I. Abrahams, *Studies in Pharisaism*, i. p. 26.
[5] Exod. xx. 12.

calling a friend 'the equal of a man's own soul.'[1] But thou dost well in making all men thy friends."

(27) He spoke kindly to him, and inquired of the 229
following one, "What is of like value with beauty?" And he said, "Piety, for this is a beauty of the first quality; and its power is love, which is God's gift. And this dost thou possess, and hast in it all blessings comprised."

(28) He applauded his answer very warmly, and 230
asked of the next how, after a failure, he should regain the esteem which he enjoyed before. And he replied, "Failure for thee is impossible, as thou hast sown the seeds of gratitude in all men, and these produce a crop of goodwill, which is mightier than the strongest armour
and affords the greatest protection. But should any 231
fail, they should no longer do those things which occasion their failure, but form friendships and act righteously. But to be a doer of good deeds and not of the contrary is a gift of God."

(29) Well pleased with this answer, he asked of the 232
next one how he might be free from grief. And he replied, "By injuring no one, doing good to all, and following after righteousness, since its fruits produce
freedom from grief. But supplication must be made to 233
God, that unforeseen accidents may not surprise and injure us, I mean such as deaths, diseases, pains and the like. But, as thou art pious, no such misfortune will surely befall thee."

(30) He commended him highly, and asked the tenth 234
man, "What is the highest form of glory?" And he said, "To honour God, and that not with gifts or sacrifices, but with purity of soul and devout conviction that all things are fashioned and directed by God in

[1] Deut. xiii. 6 (LXX text).

accordance with His will. And this is thy abiding belief, as all men may see from thy actions in the past and in the present."

235 Thereupon the king with a loud voice greeted them all and spoke kindly to them, the other guests, especially the philosophers, joining in the applause. For these men in their conduct and speech far outran the philosophers, in that they took God for their starting-point. And after this the king proceeded to shew his kindly feelings by drinking the health of his guests.

236 (31) On the following day the order of the banquet was as before, and when the king's opportunity came, he began to question the men who sat next to those who had already responded. Of the first he asked, "Can wisdom be taught?" And he replied, "The soul is so constituted that it can by divine power accept all that is good and reject what is contrary thereto."

237 (32) He expressed his assent, and inquired of the next one, "What contributes most to health?" And he said, "Temperance. But this cannot be attained unless God dispose the mind thereto."

238 (33) He gave him a kindly word, and asked of the next how one should pay his debt of gratitude to his parents. And he replied, "By giving them no pain; but this is impossible unless God becomes the mind's guide towards all that is best."

239 (34) To him also he gave his assent, and inquired of the next in order how he should become an eager listener. And he replied, "By remembering that all knowledge is profitable, since it enables thee on an emergency to select and apply some one of the things which thou hast heard and to confront the crisis,[1] with

[1] Text and meaning are doubtful.

the aid of God's guiding hand; for the fulfilment of men's actions rests with Him."

(35) He commended him, and inquired of the next 240
how he should avoid any action contrary to law. He replied thereto, "If thou wilt recognize that it is God who put the thoughts into the hearts of the lawgivers to the end that men's lives might be preserved, thou wilt become a follower of them."

(36) He approved his reply, and said to another, 241
"What advantage does kinship bring?" And he replied, "The strength of kinship is apparent if we consider that we are the losers by the misfortunes which befall *our kin*
and we make their sufferings our own. By such conduct 242
we shall win their esteem and a higher place in their regard; for an active and kindly sympathy forms of itself an indissoluble *bond* in all circumstances. But in the day of their prosperity we should crave nothing of theirs but entreat God to give *them* every blessing."

(37) He accorded a like approval to him as to the 243
others, and asked another man, "How is fearlessness attained?" And he said, "When the mind is conscious of no wrong-doing, and God directs it so that all its counsels are good."

(38) With a word of assent to him, he inquired of 244
another how he might have a right judgement always at command. He replied, "If he constantly kept the misfortunes of men before his eyes and marked how God takes away prosperity and advances others to glory and honour."

(39) He gave him his hearty approval, and requested 245
his neighbour for a reply to the question, how he might avoid a life of ease and pleasure. He replied, "By bearing always in mind that he was ruler of a great kingdom and governor of vast multitudes, and that his

mind must not be occupied with anything else, but devote its attention to their welfare. But he must ask God that none of his duties might be neglected."

246 (40) Him too he commended, and asked the tenth man how he might detect persons who were dealing treacherously with him. To this he replied, "By observing whether the bearing of those about his person was frank, and whether an orderly conduct was preserved[1] at receptions and councils and in general intercourse, and by seeing that the bounds of propriety were in no way exceeded in congratulations and in their whole
247 behaviour. But God will guide thy mind, O king, to what is best."

The king applauded and praised them all, addressing each one by name, the other guests doing likewise, and they began to make merry.[2]

248 (41) On the following day he waited for the right moment and asked the next in order, "What is the grossest negligence?" To this he replied, "When a man is careless of his children, and does not devote every effort to their education. For our prayers to God are always not so much for ourselves as for our offspring, that every blessing may be theirs. But the desire that[3] our children may be endued with sobriety comes through the power of God."

249 (42) He said that he had spoken well, and asked another how he might be a lover of his country. "By keeping in mind," he replied, "that it is good to live and die in one's own land. Residence in a foreign

[1] Or perhaps "the rule of precedence was observed."

[2] Lit. "to sing"; cf. Ecclus. xl. 20, xlix. 1.

[3] Perhaps, with the omission of one letter, "to *live to* see our children endued," etc.

country[1] brings contempt upon the poor man and disgrace on the rich, as though they were in exile for a crime. If, then, thou bestowest benefits upon all men (as is thy constant habit, since God grants thee favour with all) thou wilt be accounted a lover of thy country."

(43) After hearing him he inquired of the next one 250
how he might live amicably with *his* wife. "By bearing in mind," he replied, "that womankind are headstrong and energetic in pursuing their desires, and subject to sudden changes of opinion through fallacious reasoning, and weak by nature; and one must treat them sanely
and not by opposing provoke a quarrel. For life is then 251
guided aright, when the steersman knows the port to which he must direct his course. But, if God's help be invoked, life is indeed at all times steered aright."

(44) He admitted the wisdom of his words, and asked 252
the next one how he might be kept free from error. And he said, "By always acting with gravity[2] and deliberation, and not giving credence to slanders, but testing for thyself what is told thee, and pronouncing thy own judgement on the petitions submitted, and being guided by thy own judgement in granting them, so wilt thou be free from error, O king. But to be of this mind and to live this life is a work which demands divine power."

(45) He was delighted with these words, and asked 253
the next one how he might be free from wrath. To this he replied, "By bearing in mind that he had power to do all things, even to inflict sentence of death if he gave way to wrath; and this were unprofitable and grievous that he should deprive many of life because he was lord.

[1] Cf. the description of the humiliating life of "the sojourner" in Ecclus. xxix. 22–28.

[2] Text emended.

254 And where all were his subjects and none resisted him, to what end should he be wroth? And thou must know," he added, "that God governs the whole world with kindliness and without anger at all, and thou must follow His example, O king."

255 (46) He said that he had answered well, and inquired of him who came next, "Wherein does wise counsel consist?" "In doing all things well and with deliberation," he replied; "not neglecting in our counsels to weigh[1] the injurious effects of following the opposite view, that so after considering every point we may be well advised and our purpose may be fulfilled. But, what is more important than all, by the sovereign power of God every resolution of thine will find fulfilment, since thou dost practise piety."

256 (47) He said that he, too, had answered rightly, and asked another, "What is philosophy?" "It is to deliberate well over all contingencies," he replied, "and not to be carried away by one's impulses, but to ponder the injuries which are the outcome of the passions, and to do the duty of the moment as it should be done, practising moderation. But we must pray to God for the gift of a regard for these things."

257 (48) Him, too, he applauded, and asked another how he might meet with acceptance when travelling abroad. "By treating all men as thy equals," he said, "and behaving rather as inferior than as superior to those among whom thou sojournest. For God alike[2] accepts the lowly disposition, and the human race also deals kindly with the humble."

[1] Literally "comparing," *i. e.* with the advantages of the course adopted.

[2] Or "For it is commonly found that (it is a recognized principle that) God," etc.

(49) He expressed his assent thereto, and asked 258
another how he could so build that his structures might endure hereafter. To this he replied, "If his creations were on a great and majestic scale, so that beholders would spare them for their beauty, and if he neglected[1] no one who wrought such works, and did not compel
others to minister to his needs without pay. For if he 259
considered how God shews great consideration for the human race, supplying them with health and keenness of perception and his other gifts,[2] he himself would act likewise, by rendering to men the due reward for their arduous labours. For it is the works which are done in righteousness which also endure."

(50) He said that he, too, had spoken well, and asked 260
the tenth, "What is the fruit of wisdom?" And he replied, "To be conscious of no wrong-doing and to
live a life of sincerity. For from these things thou 261
gainest the highest joy and a tranquillity of soul, most mighty king, aye and good hopes in God, while thou dost govern thy kingdom in piety."

And all *the company* after hearing them expressed their approval with loud applause. Thereupon the king in the fulness of his joy turned to the drinking of healths.

(51) On the following day the banquet proceeded in 262
the same order as before, and when the time was come the king questioned those who yet remained. And to the first he said, "How should one keep oneself from
pride?" And he answered, "By preserving a sense of 263
equality and reminding himself on all occasions that he was a man as well as a leader of men. And God

[1] Or "dismissed."
[2] Cf. § 190.

putteth down the proud but exalteth the meek and humble."[1]

264 (52) After a kindly word to him he asked the next in order, "Whom should one take for one's counsellors?" "Those," he replied, "who had been tried in many affairs and preserved a sincere loyalty towards him, and all who shared his principles. But, that these ends may be attained, God manifests Himself to those who are worthy."

265 (53) He commended him, and asked another, "What is the most necessary possession for a king?" "The good wishes and love of his subjects," he replied. "For by these there is formed an indissoluble bond of loyalty. But it is God who causes these things to fall out as thou wouldest have them."

266 (54) He commended him highly, and inquired of another, "What is the aim of oratory?" And he said, "To convince one's opponent, pointing out his errors in an attitude of deference.[2] For in this way wilt thou win over the hearer, not by direct contradiction, but by showing appreciation withal with a view to convincing him. But persuasion is attained through God's working."

267 (55) He said that he had spoken well, and asked another how he should live amicably with the many different races within his kingdom. "By acting the proper part towards each," was his reply, "taking righteousness for thy guide, even as thou dost, since God grants thee right judgement."

268 (56) He gave him his cordial thanks, and said to the next one, "For what things should one be grieved?"

[1] Cf. 1 Sam. ii. 7 f., Prov. iii. 34, Luke i. 51 f.

[2] Such (lit. "by a subordinate position") I am now convinced is the meaning. Andrews (after Wendland) translates "in a well-ordered array *of arguments*."

To this he replied, "For our friends' misfortunes, when we see that they are protracted and irremediable. Reason does not permit us to be grieved for such as are dead and released from ills; yet all men do *so* grieve, thinking only of themselves and their own advantage. But to escape from every ill is possible only through the power of God."

(57) He said that he had answered aright, and asked 269
another, "How does ill-repute arise?" And he replied, "When pride and unbounded self-confidence lead the way, dishonour and ruined reputation follow hard on their heels. But all reputation is at God's disposal, who assigns it where He will."

(58) His reply also he endorsed, and asked the next 270
man to whom he should entrust himself. "To those," he replied, "who attend upon thee out of goodwill, and not from fear or self-interest,[1] making gain their sole motive. For the one is a token of love, but the other of illwill and time-serving; for the man who is bent on advancing his own interests is a born traitor. But thou hast the goodwill of all men, since God gives thee good counsel."

(59) He said that he had answered wisely, and said 271
to another, "What preserves a kingdom?" To this he replied, "Care and watchfulness to see that no injury is inflicted by those who are set in positions of authority over the people. And such is thy practice, since God grants thee the gift of grave reflection."

(60) He spoke encouragingly to him, and asked another, 272
"What is it that maintains favour and honour?" And he said, "Virtue, for it is the fulfilment of good works, and rejects what is base; even as thou dost preserve thy

[1] Literally "consideration," either for their own interests, or, it may be, "to gain thy consideration."

perfect bearing towards all by the gift which thou hast from God."

273 (61) He received his reply graciously, and asked the eleventh (for their number exceeded seventy by two), how even in warfare he might maintain a peaceful tranquillity of soul. And he replied, "By the consciousness of not having wronged any of thy subjects, and that all will fight in return for benefits received, knowing that even though they lay down their lives thou dost care for
274 their welfare.[1] For thou never failest to make reparation to any, such is the kindheartedness which God has given thee."

He loudly applauded and expressed his hearty approval to them all, and then drank a long draught to the health of each and gave himself up to enjoyment, sharing the men's society with merriment and high elation.

275 (62) On the seventh of the days the banquet was prepared on a larger scale, as many other visitors from the cities[2] were admitted, for a great number of ambassadors were in attendance. And when the time came the king asked the first of those who had not yet answered, how he might avoid being deceived by false reasoning.
276 And he said, "By scrutinizing the speaker and his words and the subject of his speech, and by taking time and asking the same questions in different forms. But the possession of an alert understanding and the power of passing judgement in every case is a beautiful boon of God; and this dost thou possess, O king."

277 (63) The king loudly applauded, and asked another, "Why do most men not embrace virtue?" "Because," he replied, "all men are by nature intemperate and hanker after their pleasures, by reason of which things

[1] Lit. "lives," *i.e.* their dependents. [2] Cf. § 175.

comes injustice and a sea of covetousness. But the 278
virtuous state checks those who are drifting into a life of self-indulgence and bids them prefer temperance and righteousness. But all this is under the direction of God."

(64) The king said that he had answered well, and 279
asked the next one, "Whose guidance should kings follow?" And he said, "The guidance of the laws, that so by righteous dealings they may repair the lives of men, even as thou by such action hast laid the foundation of an everlasting memorial for thyself, through following the divine commandment."

(65) He said that he also had spoken well, and asked 280
the next, "Whom should we appoint chief magistrates?"[1] And he said, "Those who have a hatred of wrong and do what is just, imitating their ruler's conduct, to the intent that they may ever be in good repute; even as thou dost," he added, "most mighty king, God having given thee a crown of righteousness."[2]

(66) He loudly signified his approval and, turning to 281
the next one, said, "Whom should we appoint as officers over the forces?" And he replied, "Those who are distinguished for bravery and justice and are more anxious for the safety of their men than to gain a victory while risking their lives in rash enterprises. For as God does good to all, so dost thou, making Him thy example, do good to thy subjects."

(67) He said that his answer was good, and asked 282
another, "What man is worthy of admiration?" And he said, "He that is endowed with glory and riches and power and yet inwardly regards himself as on an equality

[1] The reply and the succeeding question show that στρατηγός is here used of a civilian official (the governor of a district of Egypt)

[2] Cf. 2 Tim. iv. 8.

with all men, even as thou by such action art worthily admired, since God grants thee a care for these things."

283 (68) To him also he gave his assent, and said to the next, "Upon what matters should kings spend most of their time?" And he said, "In reading and *the study of* the records of official journeys,[1] which are drawn up for kings[2] with a view to the amelioration and preservation of the subjects. And by so doing thou hast won a renown beyond the reach of others, since God fulfils thy desires."

284 (69) The king spoke to him enthusiastically,[3] and asked another what he should take for his pastimes in his hours of relaxation and recreation. And he said, "To watch plays which are played with propriety and to set before one's eyes scenes from life enacted with decency and
285 restraint is profitable to one's life and appropriate. For even in these matters some instruction is contained, since often by the most insignificant of things some desirable lesson is conveyed. But thou hast practised all restraint and carriest thy philosophy into thy actions, while thou art honoured by God for thy perfect virtue."

286 (70) He was well pleased with these words, and said to the ninth, "What should be one's conduct at banquets?" And he said, "Thou shouldest invite such as are lovers of learning and able to suggest what may be useful to the kingdom and to the lives of thy subjects.[4] No more
287 harmonious or sweeter music[5] couldest thou find. For these are beloved of God, since they have trained their minds in the highest learning. And such indeed is

[1] The papyri afford examples of the diaries or *acta diurna* which officials in Egypt had to keep. Cf. § 298 *inf.*

[2] MSS "kingdoms."

[3] Text (lit. "actively," (?) = "emphatically") doubtful.

[4] Cf. on the same topic Ecclus. ix. 16, xxxi. (xxxiv.) 12 ff.

[5] Or perhaps "nothing more harmonious or educative."

thy practice, since all thy actions are directed by God."

(71) Delighted at his words, he inquired of the next 288
one, "Which is the best for the people, that a commoner should be set over them[1] as king, or one born of royal blood?" And he said, "He who has the noblest nature.
For *some* kings of royal lineage are inhuman and harsh 289
towards their subjects; and much more is this true of some who have risen from the ranks, who after experiencing misery and a taste of poverty have, on becoming rulers of multitudes, proved themselves more cruel than
the unholy tyrants. But, as I said before, a good dis- 290
position which has had the advantage of culture is fitted to bear rule, even as thou art a great king, not so much through the pre-eminent glory of thy rule and thy wealth, as because thou hast outstripped all men in gentleness and kindness, since God has conferred these gifts upon thee."

(72) He commended him at some length,[2] and asked 291
him who was last of all, "What is the greatest achievement in the office of a king?" To this he replied, "If his subjects enjoy continual peace and get speedy justice
done them when their cases are tried. And these results 292
follow when the governor is a hater of evil and a lover of good and makes much of the saving of a man's life; even as thou regardest injustice as the greatest of evils, and by thy just government in all things hast procured for thyself an imperishable renown, since God vouchsafes to give thee a pure mind untainted with evil."

When his speech was ended, there was a burst of 293
applause with shouting and jubilation lasting for a good

[1] Text emended: MSS "appointed by them."

[2] Possibly the words "during a long time" should be attached to the preceding speech.

while. And when this ceased, the king took a goblet and drank a toast in honour of all his guests and the speeches which they had delivered. And in conclusion he said, "You have brought me the greatest of blessings
294 by your coming, for I have derived great benefit from the doctrine which you have laid down to guide me in my kingly office." And he commanded that to each should be given three talents of silver and the slave who should hand it to him. All the guests shouted their approval and the banquet become a scene of rejoicing, while the king gave himself up to a continuous round of festivity.

295 Now, if I have been too prolix,[1] dear Philocrates, I pray thee to excuse this fault. For I admired beyond measure the way in which the men on the spur of the moment were ready with their replies which required much
296 meditation; and, seeing that their interrogator had carefully thought out each question, while the respondents one after the other had the task of replying thereto, they did indeed appear to me and to those who were present, but chiefly to the philosophers, deserving of admiration. And I believe that to all into whose hands this narrative
297 may come it will appear incredible. But to be untruthful in matters which are reported in the public archives is not meet. Were I even to pass over anything, it would be an act of impiety where such matters are concerned. No, we describe just what took place, conscientiously disclaiming all error. To this end, so much was I impressed with their powers of speech, I endeavoured to obtain information from those persons who record in detail all that takes place at the king's
298 audiences and entertainments. For it is the custom, as thou art aware, to have a record kept of all that is said

[1] Text emended.

and done from the hour when the king begins to give audience until he retires to rest, and the practice is a good and useful one. The next day, before any audience 299
is given, the minutes of the doings and sayings of the previous day are read through, and any irregularity which has occurred is corrected. We have, then, as we said, 300
obtained accurate information on all points from the public records,[1] and have set it down here in writing, knowing as we did thy love of useful learning.

(X) THE TRANSLATION AND ITS RECEPTION

Now after three days Demetrius took the men with 301
him and passing over the break-water,[2] seven furlongs[3] in length, to the island crossed the bridge and proceeded to the northern district. There he held a session in a nouse which had been prepared by the sea-shore, magnificently built in a secluded situation, and bade them carry out their work of translation, since all the necessary appliances had been well provided. And so they pro- 302
ceeded to carry it out, arriving at an agreement on each point by comparing each other's work; the appropriate rendering so agreed on was then transcribed under the direction of Demetrius. The session used to last until 303
the ninth hour, and thereafter they would depart to attend to their bodily comforts, all their wants being plentifully supplied. Moreover, Dorotheus[4] used every 304
day to make the same arrangements for them as were made for the king, for he had the king's order so to do. Every day at dawn they would come to the court, make

[1] Or "from the keepers of the public records." The text is slightly emended.

[2] For the island of Pharos and the Heptastadion which connected it with the mainland see Strabo xvii. 6 (792).

[3] Gr. "stades."

[4] Cf. § 182.

their salutation to the king and depart to their own place.
305 And when, as is the custom of all the Jews, they had
washed their hands in the sea and had offered a prayer
to God, they betook themselves to the reading and
306 interpretation of each passage.—I questioned them on
this point, why it was that they washed their hands before
praying. And they explained that it was in token that
they had done no wrong, since the hands are the medium
for all activity; in such a beautiful and pious spirit do
they make all things symbols of righteousness and truth.—
307 Thus, as we have said already, they assembled every day
in this spot, which the peacefulness and brilliant light
rendered so delightful, and carried on their appointed
task. And so it came about that the translation[1] was
accomplished in seventy-two days, as though this
coincidence had been intended.

308 And when the work was ended, Demetrius assembled
the Jewish people on the spot where the translation had
been made and read it through to the whole assembly
in the presence of the translators, who received another
great ovation from the people in recognition of the great
309 services which they had rendered. And they gave a
similar reception to Demetrius and requested him to
have a copy of the whole Law transcribed and to present
310 it to their rulers. And after the reading of the rolls
the priests and the elders of the translators and some
members of the *Jewish* community and the rulers of the
people stood up and said, "Forasmuch as the translation
has been well and piously executed and with perfect
accuracy, it is right that it should remain in its present
311 form and that no revision should take place." And when
all had assented to these words, they[2] bade them, in

[1] Lit. "transcription."
[2] Or, according to another reading, "he (Demetrius) bade them."

accordance with their custom, pronounce an imprecation upon any who should revise the text by adding to, or in any way transposing,[1] or omitting ought from, what had been written;[2] and herein they did well, to the intent that the work might for ever be preserved imperishable and unchanged.

When word of these proceedings was brought to the 312
king, he greatly rejoiced, for it seemed that his purpose
had been securely attained. The whole work was read
through to him, and he was greatly astonished at the
spirit of the lawgiver. And he said to Demetrius, "How
is it that none of the historians or poets ever thought of
mentioning such great achievements?" And he said, 313
"Because the Law is holy and has been given by God;
and some of those who did essay to do so were smitten
of God and desisted from their attempt." For he said 314
that he had heard Theopompus[3] tell how when he was
too rashly intending to introduce into his history some
of the incidents from the Law which had previously been
translated,[4] his mind was deranged for more than thirty
days; and when the disorder abated he besought God
that the cause of the misfortune might be made plain to
him; and when it was shewn him in a dream that his 315
desire to disclose divine truths to common men was
misguided, he desisted, and thereupon recovered his

[1] Or "altering."

[2] Cf. Deut. iv. 2, xii. 32, and for the imprecation Rev. xxii. 18 f.

[3] Theopompus, the historian, lived from about 378 to 300 B.C. About 305 B.C. he came to Egypt, but was not in favour with Ptolemy I, who would have put him to death as a dangerous busybody had not his friends interceded for his life. It is interesting to compare this with the statement in Aristeas as to his meddling with divine matters, although the incident here related has probably no foundation in fact.

[4] Or perhaps "when he was intending to introduce . . some of the incidents from the Law which had previously been translated in a somewhat misleading way" (cf. § 30).

316 reason. "I have been informed too," *he added*, "by Theodectes,[1] the tragic poet, that when he was intending to introduce into one of his plays something recorded in the Book,[2] he was afflicted with cataract of the eyes; and, suspecting that this was the reason for his mishap, he besought God's mercy and after many days recovered his sight."

(XI) THE DEPARTURE OF THE TRANSLATORS

317 The king, when he heard the explanation which Demetrius gave of this matter, as above narrated, made obeisance, and ordered that great care should be taken of the books, and that they should be guarded with
318 proper awe. He further besought the translators that after their return to Judaea they would visit him very often. It was but right, he added, that they should now be sent home, but, should they visit him, he would in bounden duty treat them as friends, and they would
319 meet with the utmost consideration[3] at his hands. He ordered preparations to be made for their sending off and treated the men munificently. To each one he gave three of the finest changes of raiment, and two talents of gold, and a side-board[4] of a talent *in weight*, and all the furniture for the three couches of a dining-
320 room. To Eleazar also he sent by the hands of their escort ten couches with legs of silver and all the appurtenances thereof and a side-board[4] of thirty talents and

[1] Theodectes, a rhetorician and tragic poet, a contemporary and on one occasion a rival of Theopompus, circa 375–334 B.C.

[2] This seems to be the earliest use of ἡ βίβλος for a collection of sacred writings.

[3] Text slightly emended: MSS "receive rich presents," perhaps rightly (cf. App. p. 103).

[4] Or "cupboard" in its literal sense (1 Macc. xv. 32). The MSS, omitting one letter, read "a small cup."

ten changes of raiment and a purple robe and a magnificent crown and a hundred pieces of fine woven linen and vials and dishes and two golden bowls as a dedicatory offering. He wrote a letter also requesting him that if 321
any of the men should choose to return to him he would not prevent them from so doing; for he counted it a privilege to enjoy the society of learned men, and would rather lavish his wealth upon such persons than upon vanities.

(XII) CONCLUDING ADDRESS TO PHILOCRATES

There, Philocrates, thou hast the whole story which 322
I promised thee. And indeed I believe that thou findest greater pleasure in these matters than in the books of the romancers;[1] for thou art devoted to the study of those things which can profit the mind and art at most times occupied therewith. I shall, moreover, attempt to put on record whatever else is worthy of narration, that by the perusal thereof thou mayest win the fairest reward for thy zealous desire.

[1] Or "mythologists."

APPENDIX

THE EVIDENCE OF SOME ANCIENT JEWISH AND CHRISTIAN WRITERS ON THE ORIGIN OF THE SEPTUAGINT VERSION.

(A) **Jewish (Rabbinic).**

(1) MEGILLATH TAANITH (The "Roll of Fasting").

[The calendar of Fast-days and Festivals seems to have originated in Maccabaean times, but received later additions from time to time. The present passage occurs in an appendix of fasts in Neubauer's edition, *Anecdota Oxoniensia*, *Semitic Series*, vol. i, part vi, *Mediaeval Jewish Chronicles* ii, Oxford 1895.]

On the eighth [1] *day* of Tebeth [2] the Law was written [3] in Greek in the days of King Tolmai,[4] and darkness [5] came upon the world for three days.

(2) MASSEKETH SOPHERIM ("The Tractate of the Scribes"), I. 7–10 (ed. Joel Müller, Leipzig, 1878).

[A post-Talmudic treatise on the rules for writing the rolls of the Law and kindred matters. Though not earlier than the eighth or ninth century A.D., it includes

[1] One Oxford MS reads "seventh."
[2] The tenth month in the Jewish year (=December–January).
[3] Mere transliteration of the Hebrew in Greek characters, not translation, *may* be intended.
[4] Ptolemy. [5] Lit. "the darkness"; cf. Ex. x. 21 f.

much ancient matter. The first of the two narratives below, with its unique reference to the *five* (instead of the usual seventy or seventy-two elders) bears the marks of high antiquity; the second is of later origin and finds parallels in the two Talmuds and elsewhere. Of the thirteen or more passages in the Law, cited in this and the two following extracts, which are said to have been altered by the elders, four only appear in the "altered" form in our MSS of the LXX; two more of the variants are attested in African versions. Of the remainder, some are unmistakably, and all may be, mere variants in a *Hebrew* text; and it has been suggested (Frankel, *Vorstudien* 31) that they were originally cited as readings in the *Hebrew* codex of the Law presented to King Ptolemy, not in a Greek translation made from that codex.]

7 *The Law* must not be written in *ordinary* Hebrew[1] nor in Aramaic nor in the Median language nor in Greek. A copy written in any *foreign* tongue or *foreign* characters shall not be used for reading *in the services*, but only one written in the Assyrian characters.[2]

8 It happened once that five elders[3] wrote[4] the Law in Greek for King Tolmai; and that day was a hard day for Israel, like the day on which Israel made the *golden* calf,[5] because the Law was not capable of being interpreted according to all its requirements.

[1] The older and "common Semitic character used alike in ancient times by the Moabites, Hebrews, Aramaeans and Phoenicians" (Driver, *Notes on the Heb. text of Samuel*, Introd. § 1).

[2] The later square Hebrew characters.

[3] One MS "they wrote," omitting "five elders." Frankel (*Ueber den Einfluss der paläst. Exegese*) thinks that we have here a true tradition and that it is confirmed by indications, which he finds in the LXX text, that each book of the Pentateuch was rendered by a separate translator. Grätz adopts this theory.

[4] This might refer to mere transcription of the Hebrew text in Greek characters.

[5] Ex. xxxii.

Again, it happened to King Tolmai that he as- 9
sembled seventy[1] elders and placed them in seventy[1]
cells,[2] and did not make known to them wherefore he
had assembled them; *but* he came in to each of them
in turn and said to them, "Write me out the Law of
Moses your master." God put counsel into the heart
of every one of them, that they were all of one mind,
and they wrote out for him the Law by itself.[3] But
they altered thirteen[4] passages in it, and they are
these:[5]—

(1) "God created in the beginning":[6]

(2) "And God said, I will make man in image and in likeness":[7]

(3) "And he finished on the sixth *day* and rested on the seventh":[8]

(4) "Male and female created he him":[9]

(5) "Go to, let me go down and there confound their language":[10]

[1] *v.l.* "seventy-two."

[2] Lit. "houses."

[3] The writer emphasizes the limitation of their task to the Law alone.

[4] Actually fourteen are cited. No. (10), omitted in the Jerus. Talmud, may be a later addition.

[5] The last four words are omitted in some MSS.

[6] Gen. i. 1; instead of the order "In the beginning created God," etc. The divine name occupies the first place. LXX keeps the usual order and, except as indicated, the normal text in the passages which follow.

[7] Gen. i. 26; instead of "Let *us* make . . . in *our* image, after *our* likeness." The polytheistic plural is avoided.

[8] Gen. ii. 2; so LXX, instead of "And on the *seventh* day God finished his work," etc. Text due to Sabbatarian scruples.

[9] Gen. i. 27, v. 2; instead of "created he them," which words are omitted by one Egyptian version of LXX (the Bohairic). Tradition said that the first man, before the creation of Eve, was of double sex and had two faces.

[10] Gen. xi. 7; instead of "Let us go down." Polytheistic plural again avoided.

(6) "And Sarah laughed within herself saying": [1]

(7) "For in their anger they slew an ox, and in their self-will they uprooted a stall": [2]

(8) "And Moses took his wife and his sons and set them upon a bearer of men": [3]

(9) "Now the sojourning of the children of Israel, which they sojourned in the land of Egypt and in the land of Canaan and in the rest of the lands, was four hundred and thirty years": [4]

(10) "And upon the *Zaṭuṭim* of the children of Israel he laid not his hand": [5]

(11) "I have not taken one desirable thing from them": [6]

(12) "And the short-footed one": [7]

(13) "Which the LORD thy God hath divided to

[1] Gen. xviii. 12; a mere difference by one letter in the spelling of the Hebrew word "laughed," perhaps to distinguish Sarah's laughter from Abraham's (Gen. xvii. 17).

[2] Gen. xlix. 6; for "they slew *a man*, . . . they houghed an ox." The alteration, made from a desire to clear Levi of man-slaughter, has perhaps affected the Ethiopic version of LXX ("cities" for "an ox"). "A stall"; *'ēbûs*. Friedmann suggests an allusion to Apis and Egyptian idolatry.

[3] Ex. iv. 20; for ". . . upon an ass." Alteration from regard to Moses' dignity. LXX "upon the beasts of burden."

[4] Ex. xii. 40; "and in the land of Canaan and in the rest of the lands" inserted on chronological grounds. LXX has part of this, "and in the land of Canaan," with the further addition (in many MSS) "they and their fathers."

[5] Ex. xxiv. 11; for "And upon the *nobles*," etc. The Hebrew word occurs here only in this sense, lit. "corners," so "supports." The meaning of *Zaṭuṭim* is obscure; probably it is a transliteration of the Gr. *zêtêtai* (= "commissioners") or *zaetêtai* = *diaetêtai* ("arbitrators"). LXX ("the elect") does not help to explain it.

[6] Numb. xvi. 15; for "one ass." LXX has this variant, "desirable thing"; the Hebrew word differs from "ass" by a slight change in one letter.

[7] Read, with a change of one letter, "the hairy-footed one." Deut. xiv. 7 (cf. Lev. xi. 5 f), "and the hare" (*hâ-arnebeth*); LXX "the hairy-foot" (*dasupoda*), the later Greek name for the hare instead of the classical word *lagôs*. See further on this word below.

give light unto all the peoples under the whole heaven": [1]

(14) "Which I have not commanded *them* to serve": [2]

They do not write *the Law* in gold *letters*. It hap- 10
pened in the case of the copy of their Law which went to them of Alexandria [3] that all the *divine* names [4] were written in gold; and when the matter came before the Wise, they said, "Put it away." [5]

(3) TALMUD OF JERUSALEM (PALESTINIAN TALMUD), Megilla I. 71 d (bottom) (cf. *Mechilta* on Exod. xii. 40).

Thirteen passages were altered by the Wise for King Tolmai. They wrote *thus* for him.

[Then follow the passages cited in the previous extract, except that No. (10) is omitted; the order of Nos. (3) and (4) is transposed, as also of (11) and (12). No. (12), here No. (10), appears in the following form:—]

And *for* "the hare" [*hâ-arnebeth*] *they wrote* "the short-footed one"; [6] the name of the mother of King Tolmai was Arnabtha. [7]

(4) TALMUD OF BABYLON, Megilla 9a.

[The preceding Mishna, after stating that the books of Scripture may be written in any foreign language,

[1] Deut. iv. 19. The words "to give light" are added to emphasize the fact that the luminaries were not given to be worshipped.

[2] Deut. xvii. 3. The addition of the words "to serve" is similar to that in the previous passage; it appears in one Egyptian version made from the LXX, the Bohairic (*facere*).

[3] Another reading "to Alexander."

[4] Lit. "mentions," "allusions" (to the Name).

[5] *i.e.* in the Geniza, or synagogue lumber-room, as unfit for use in the services. Cf. Aristeas, § 176, where the whole of the MS is said to have been written in gold.

[6] Read "the hairy-footed one"; see above.

[7] See note on the next extract.

adds the stricter ruling of Rabbi Simon ben Gamaliel hat they might be written only in Greek.]

Rabbi Jehuda said that the permission of our Rabbis as to *writing in* Greek extends only to the book of the Law, and that because of what happened in the case of King Tolmai. We are taught thus :—[1]

It happened to King Tolmai that he assembled seventy-two elders and collected them in seventy-two cells[2] and did not reveal to them wherefore he had assembled them; but he came in to each of them in turn and said to them, "Write me out the Law of Moses your master." The Holy One (blessed be He!) put counsel into the heart of every one of them, that they were all of one mind, and they wrote for him *as follows*.

[Then follow the fourteen passages quoted in *Masseketh Sopherim* (above), to which is added a fifteenth, between Nos. (9) and (10), viz. :—]

> "And he sent the *Zaṭuṭim* of the children of Israel."[3]

[Other variations from *Mas. Soph.* are that to passage (4) the note is added "And they did not write, 'He created them'": in passage (9) the words "and in the land of Canaan" are not inserted, and the number of the years is, in some MSS, 400: and passage (12), which here occupies the fifteenth and final place, appears in the following expanded form :—]

> "And they wrote for him 'the short-footed one,' and they did not write for him 'the hare' [*hâ-arnebeth*], because of the wife of Tolmai, whose name was Arnebeth, lest he should say, 'The Jews have

[1] *i. e.* "There is a tradition" (outside the Mishna).
[2] Lit. "houses."
[3] Ex. xxiv. 5; for "And he sent young men," etc. For *Zaṭuṭim* see note on passage (10) under *Mas. Soph.* (above).

mocked me by introducing the name of my wife into the Law.'"[1]

(B) **Jewish (Hellenistic).**

(5) (PSEUDO-)ARISTOBULUS, as cited by Eusebius, *Preparation for the Gospel*, XIII. 12.

[The work, of which this fragment, with a few others, has survived, consisted of an allegorical and philosophical explanation of the Mosaic Law. It purports to have been addressed to King Ptolemy Philometor (182–146 B.C.), but its claim to so high an antiquity has, like that of the Letter of Aristeas, been disputed by many recent critics.]

It is evident that Plato was a follower of our code of laws, evident too that he diligently studied all their details. For before the time of Demetrius of Phalerum, before the dominion of Alexander and of the Persians, a translation had been made by others of the narrative of the leading forth of the Hebrews, our fellow countrymen,[2] out of Egypt, and of the *divine* manifestation in all which befell them, and of the occupation of the *promised* land,

[1] We have here a curious distortion of an older story attaching to the LXX word for "hare" (*dasupous*, "hairy-foot"). Doubtless the original explanation was that the translators avoided the classical word, *lagôs*, for the unclean animal, because it might be construed as a reflection on the name of Lagos, the father of Ptolemy I, and on the dynasty of the Lagidae. The story was forgotten and another confused explanation took its place. *Sopherim* gives the LXX rendering without comment; in the Jerusalem Talmud the king's father is replaced by his mother, and she again in the Bab. Talmud by his wife, and the point of the story is now found apparently in a resemblance between the *Hebrew* word for "hare,' *arnebeth*, and the royal name Arsinoe.

[2] Lit. "(fellow-)citizens."

with a detailed statement of the entire Law.[1] It is thus abundantly clear that the aforesaid philosopher has derived many things *therefrom*; for he was a man of great learning, like Pythagoras, who also borrowed many of our doctrines and incorporated them in his decrees. But the complete translation of the Law and all its contents was made under the king surnamed Philadelphus, thy[2] ancestor, who displayed the greatest zeal,[3] while Demetrius of Phalerum busied himself with the necessary arrangements.

(6) PHILO, *On the Life of Moses*, II. 5–7.

5 The admiration in which the reverend Law has been held, not by Jews alone but also by the rest of the world, is evident alike from what has already been said and from the story which I proceed to tell. In the olden days the laws were written in the Chaldee[4] tongue, and for a long while so they continued without any change in their language, when as yet they had not displayed their beauty to the rest of men. But when, through the constant daily study and practice of these laws by their followers, others also awoke to a knowledge of them, and their fame spread far and wide—for beautiful objects, though for a while they may be obscured through envy, by a kindly law of nature again in due season recover their brilliance—certain persons feeling aggrieved that the laws should find a place with half only, the non-Hellenic[5] portion, of the human race, while the Hellenic half should have no share in them whatever, applied

[1] The alleged pre-Septuagint version is represented as comprising at least portions of the last five books of the Hexateuch.

[2] Ptolemy VII (Philometor) is addressed.

[3] Or "greater ambition" (viz. than the earlier translators).

[4] *i.e.* Hebrew. Philo uses the words "Chaldaean" and "Hebrew" indiscriminately.

[5] Lit. "barbarian."

themselves to their translation. And since the task was great and for the general good, it was entrusted not to common folk nor to *ordinary* rulers, whose number is legion, but to kings and to the most notable among them. Ptolemy, surnamed Philadelphus, was the third *in the dynasty which dated* from Alexander [1] the conqueror of Egypt, and in the kingly virtues surpassed not only the monarchs of his time but all who ever were before him. To this very day, so many generations later, the fame is sung of him who left, throughout cities and countries, such abundant evidences and memorials of his magnanimity, insomuch that it has now become almost a proverbial saying to describe acts of exceeding munificence and buildings on a mighty scale, after his name, as "Philadelphian." In short, the house of the Ptolemies flourished above all other kingdoms, and among the Ptolemies Philadelphus *ranked highest.* The united achievements of all the rest hardly equalled the laudable deeds of this one monarch; he was like the directing mind in a living organism, the head, as it were, of the kingly body.

Such, then, was the man who, conceiving a passion- 6
ate desire for our code of laws, proposed to have the Chaldee [2] rendered into the Greek tongue, and straightway sent ambassadors unto the high priest and king of Judaea (for the same man held both offices) to declare his will and to exhort him to select according to their merits persons to translate the Law. And he, with natural delight and supposing that the king's zeal for so high a task was not uninspired by divine providence, looked out the most approved of the Hebrews who were with him, men who had been trained in the Hellenic

[1] Lit. "third from Alexander," *i. e.* his second successor.
[2] *i. e.* Hebrew (as above).

learning in addition to that of their country,[1] and gladly despatched them. On their arrival they were invited to a banquet and entertained and feasted their host in return with clever and earnest speeches.[2] For he made trial of each man's wisdom, propounding novel and unusual questions, while they, the occasion not permitting of a long discourse, solved the conundrums which were put to them with the ready sagacity and pointed repartee of the speaker of terse apophthegms.

After passing this scrutiny, they proceeded straightway to discharge the duties of their honourable embassy; and reflecting with one another upon the magnitude of the task of giving an oracular interpretation of divinely inspired laws, being under constraint neither to detract ought nor to add nor to transpose,[3] but to preserve their original form and type, they looked for the purest spot in the district, without the city. For the parts within the walls, being full of living creatures of all sorts, were, by reason of diseases and deaths and the unholy actions of those in sound health, viewed with suspicion. The island of Pharos lies in front of Alexandria; its neck of land with half-submerged sandbanks stretches along over against the city and is washed by a sea which is not deep close inshore but for the most part consists of lagoons, so that the mighty roar and crash of the waves breaking a very great distance away are deadened. This spot out of all the surrounding district they selected as the most suitable haven wherein to find peace and quietness and for solitary communion between their souls and the laws. So here they abode, and taking the holy books they extended their hands with them to heaven, entreating God that they might not fail in their purpose. And He

[1] Cf. Arist. § 121. Philo, it is to be observed, names no number.
[2] Arist. §§ 187 ff.
[3] Cf. Arist. § 310 f.

granted their prayers, in order that the more part, or indeed the whole, of the human race might reap the benefit of access, for the amendment of life, to *our* wise[1] and wholly excellent ordinances.

In secret they sat, with none present save the 7
elements of nature—earth, water, air, heaven—whose origin it was their first task to expound (for the cosmogony holds the first place in our laws); and, as men possessed, they produced not divers interpretations, but all alike used the same words and phrases, as though some invisible prompter whispered in the ears of each. And yet who does not know that every language, and Greek beyond all others, is rich in words and that one may by circumlocution and paraphrase clothe the same thought in divers forms, varying the style to fit the occasion? Yet this, they say, did not happen with these laws *of ours*; no, the appropriate technical words *in the translation* corresponded exactly with the technical words *in the original*, the Greek with the Chaldee,[2] being admirably adapted to fit the subject-matter. Just in the same way, I suppose, as in geometry and dialectics, the meanings *of the terms used* do not admit of any variety of definition, but that which is laid down in the first instance is retained throughout, so, it seems, these men discovered the words which coincided with the subject-matter and which were alone, or most nearly, capable of rendering the sense transparently clear. The surest proof of the foregoing statement is this. If Chaldaeans[2] learn Greek or Greeks Chaldee[2] and they read both writings, the Chaldee[2] and the translation, they are filled with amazement and veneration for what appear as sister writings or rather as one and the same work

[1] Lit. "philosophical."
[2] *i.e.* Hebrew (Hebrews).

as regards both subject-matter and phraseology, and they call those men not translators but priests of the mysteries and prophets, to whom it was vouchsafed with sincerity of mind to enter into[1] the spotlessly pure spirit of Moses.

For this cause there is held to this day every year a festival and public assembly on the island of Pharos, to which not Jews only but multitudes from other nations cross the water, to pay reverence to the spot on which the translation first shed its light, and to give thanks to God for a benefit, ancient yet ever new. After the prayers and thanksgivings some pitch tents on the sea-shore, while others recline on the sand, and all keep feast in the open with relatives and friends, regarding the beach on that occasion as more luxurious than a royal palace. So desirable and highly to be prized do our laws appear to all alike, whether commoners or rulers, and that though for a long time the fortunes of the race have been at a low ebb, and nations that are not at their prime are wont to suffer eclipse. If, then, there should come an opening to a brighter future, what an advance may we not hope will be made?[2] I suppose that all nations would forsake their own *customs* and bidding farewell to their country's *laws* would come to pay honour to these laws alone; for with the revival of the nation's fortunes they will recover their brilliance and rob all others of their brightness even as the sun at his rising blots out the stars.

(7) Josephus

(*a*) *Jewish Antiquities*, I. 3 (§§ 10–12, Niese).

I found that the second of the Ptolemies, a king who was zealous beyond all others in the cause of learning

[1] Lit. "run (*or* keep pace) with." [2] Cf. Rom. xi. 12.

and in the collecting of books, had a special ambition to produce a version in the Greek tongue of our Law and the polity which is ordered in accordance therewith. I found too that Eleazar, who came behind none of our high priests in virtue, did not grudge the aforesaid king the enjoyment of this benefit, which he would doubtless have denied him, had it not been the custom of our nation to keep no good thing a secret to themselves. I considered accordingly that it became me also to imitate the high priest's magnanimity and to suppose that even now there are many who share the king's love of learning. For even he did not obtain the whole record and so forestall *me*, since it was the Law alone which was delivered *him* by those who were sent to Alexandria as interpreters.

(*b*) *Ib.* XII. 2. 1 (§ 11).

Alexander reigned twelve years, and after him Ptolemy Soter forty-one years, and then Philadelphus succeeded to the throne of Egypt and occupied it for thirty-nine years. He translated the Law and liberated from bondage those of the inhabitants of Jerusalem who were bondsmen in Egypt, in number about one hundred and twenty thousand, on the following grounds.

[Then follows a free paraphrase of a large part of the Letter of Aristeas.]

(C) **Christian.**

(8) JUSTIN, *Apology*, I. 31.

Now when Ptolemy, the king of the Egyptians, was forming a library and endeavoured to make a collection of all men's writings, he heard tell, among the rest, of these prophecies, and sent to Herod who was then king of the Jews with a request that the books of the prophecies might be transmitted to him. And king Herod sent them, written in their native Hebrew tongue of which I have spoken. But, since the Egyptians were unacquainted with the things written therein, he sent yet again and requested him to despatch men to render them into the Greek language. This was done and the books remained with the Egyptians and are there to this day.

(9) PSEUDO-JUSTIN, *Exhortation to Greeks*, 13.

Ptolemy, king of Egypt, formed a library in Alexandria and collected books from every quarter and filled it. Then, learning that certain ancient histories written in Hebrew characters had been preserved with scrupulous care, and being desirous to know what was written therein, he sent to Jerusalem for seventy wise men, who were familiar with the speech of both Greeks and Hebrews, and bade them translate the books. And, in order that they should be free from all disturbance and the sooner complete their task, he gave orders for their accommodation not in the city itself, but seven furlongs[1] away, where the Pharos[2] was built, and that little cells, in number as many as the translators, should be erected there, to the end that every man should execute his translation apart by himself. He charged the attendant ministers to see that they wanted for nothing, but to keep them from communicating with each other, in order that their agreement might afford a further proof of the accuracy of the translation. When he found that the seventy men had not merely expressed the same ideas but had employed the very same phraseology, and had not so much as in a single word failed to agree with each other, but had written on the same themes in the same language, he

[1] Gr. "stades," [2] *i.e.* the lighthouse on the island.

was amazed, and, believing that the translation had been written by divine power, he recognized that they merited every honour, as men beloved of God. So he bestowed many presents[1] upon them and bade them return to their own country; the books, as he was like to do,[2] he held to be divine and laid up in his library.

These things which we declare unto you, men of Greece, are no myths nor fictitious history. We ourselves have been in Alexandria and have seen the traces, still preserved, of the cells in the island of Pharos, and have heard this story which we tell you from the inhabitants, who have had it handed down as a tradition of their country. You may learn it from others also, and chiefly from those wise and distinguished men who have written of it, Philo and Josephus, but there are many others besides.

(10) IRENAEUS, *Against all Heresies*, III. xxi. 2.

Before the Romans had established their empire and when the Macedonians were still masters of Asia, Ptolemy son of Lagus, in his ambition to adorn the library which he had built in Alexandria with the writings of all men, such at least as were of merit, besought of the inhabitants of Jerusalem that he might have their Scriptures rendered into the Greek tongue. And they, being at that time still subject to the Macedonians, sent of their number those who were most proficient in the Scriptures and in both languages, seventy elders, to Ptolemy to do his will.[3] The king, desiring to make trial of them privily, and fearing lest by some mutual covenant

[1] Cf. Arist. § 318 (with the MS reading).

[2] Or, "as was meet."

[3] Or, according to another reading, "God having wrought that which he desired."

they might through their translation conceal the truth contained in the Scriptures, separated them from each other and commanded the whole company to translate the same portion of Scripture; and this he did with all the books. Now when they were assembled together in Ptolemy's presence and compared every man his translation *with his neighbour's*, God was glorified, and the Scriptures were recognized as indeed divine, in that they had all expressed the same things by the same phrases and the same words from beginning to end, insomuch that even the Gentiles who were present perceived that the Scriptures had been translated through the inspiration of God. . . .

4 For it was one and the self-same Spirit of God, who in the prophets proclaimed what and in what manner should be the coming of the Lord and in the elders interpreted well what had been well prophesied.

(11) CLEMENT OF ALEXANDRIA, *Stromateis*, I, § 148 (409 P.).

[Based on Irenaeus, or a common source, and Aristobulus.]

They say that the Scriptures, both of the Law and of the prophets, were translated from the Hebrew tongue into Greek under King Ptolemy, son of Lagus, or, as some assert, under him who was surnamed Philadelphus, Demetrius of Phalerum displaying the greatest zeal in this undertaking and carefully supervising the details of the business. It was in the days when the Macedonians were still masters of Asia that the king was fired with the ambition to adorn the library which he had founded in Alexandria with all manner of writings, and among other requests asked the men of Jerusalem to translate the prophecies in their keeping into the Greek tongue.

And they, being still subject to the Macedonians, 149
selected from the most renowned among them seventy elders, skilled in the Scriptures and acquainted with the Greek language, and sent them to him with the sacred books. Each man in turn and apart translated each several prophecy, and all the translations when compared conspired together both in thought and diction; †for the will of God had been[1] attuned to[2]† Greek ears. And surely it was not strange that the inspiration of God who had given the prophecy operated to make of the translation also as it were a Greek prophecy; seeing that, when the Scriptures had perished in the captivity under Nebuchadnezzar, in the days of Artaxerxes, the king of the Persians, Esdras the Levite and priest was inspired to revive and to prophesy afresh all the ancient Scriptures.

(12) TERTULLIAN, *Apology*, 18.

The most erudite of the Ptolomies, whom they surname Philadelphus, and one who was most deeply versed in all literature, when in his passion for collecting books he was, I suppose, emulating Pisistratus, among other records whose title to fame was due to their antiquity or some curious lore, besought the Jews also for their own literature, of which they were the sole possessors, in its native tongue. This he did on the suggestion of Demetrius of Phalerum, the most eminent philologist of his time, to whom he had entrusted the superintendence of the volumes. For at all times prophets had arisen from among them and had pleaded with them, as being a nation who in virtue of the favour shown to their fathers were God's own peculiar people. Those who

[1] Wendland emends "for by the will of God they [the translations] had been," etc.

[2] Or "studied" or "rehearsed for." Meaning of †† doubtful.

are now Jews were once Hebrews, and consequently had their Hebrew characters [1] and language. To guard, however, against misunderstanding, Ptolomy had further placed at his disposal by the Jews the services of two and seventy translators, whom even the philosopher Menedemus, the upholder of Providence, regarded with esteem on account of the opinion which they held in common with himself.[2] You have confirmation in this in what Aristaeus has stated. Thus *the king* left the records in Greek and accessible to all.[3] To this day the libraries of Ptolomy are shewn in the Serapeum with the actual Hebrew documents.

(13) ANATOLIUS, *Canons concerning the Passover* (as quoted by Eusebius, *Eccles. Hist.*, VII. 32).

[The writer, an Alexandrian by birth, and in the latter part of the third century bishop of the Syrian Laodicea, among other authorities on the method of calculating the time of the Passover, mentions]

The famous Aristobulus, who was enrolled among the Seventy who translated the holy and divine Scriptures of the Hebrews for Ptolemy Philadelphus and his father; he also addressed to those same kings books in which he expounded the meaning of the Mosaic law.

(14) EUSEBIUS, *Preparation for the Gospel*, VIII. 1.

Before calling my witnesses, I think it necessary to explain to my readers how the oracles of the Hebrews passed into Greek hands, the manner of the translation of the divine Scriptures with which that nation had been entrusted, the number and nature of the translators, and the royal zeal which brought about the version into the

[1] Or "literature."

[2] Cf. Arist. § 201.

[3] The sentence might possibly mean "He (*i. e.* Aristeas) has left records to this effect in Greek," etc.

Greek tongue. The narrative will not fail to contribute to my demonstration of the Preparation for the Gospel.

When the time was close at hand in which, under the Roman Empire, the salutary preaching concerning our Saviour was destined to shed forth its light upon all men, and there was thus an exceptional and imperative reason why the prophecies concerning Him and the life of the divinely favoured Hebrews of old and the lessons of their pious teaching, which for long ages had been veiled in their country's language, should now at length be transmitted to all the nations, who were to be introduced to the privileges of a knowledge of God, God Himself, the author of these benefits, anticipating the future with divine foreknowledge, providentially ordained that the predictions about Him Who was shortly to appear as Saviour of all men and to become for all nations under the sun the Teacher of pious worship of the one supreme God, should, by means of an accurate version deposited in public libraries, be revealed to the world and come to light. It was King Ptolemy into whose heart He put it to fulfil this task, in preparation, it would seem, for the impending time when all nations would participate in these blessings.

For to those treasures which we should not otherwise have wrested from the Jews, who through envy of us would have concealed their oracles, to these we gained access through the translation, dispensed by divine providence and executed by men who for wisdom and learning in their country's lore were held in high repute by their nation.

The story is told by Aristaeus, a man of exceptional erudition, who moreover took part in the events which happened under the second Ptolemy, surnamed Philadelphus. For it was in his reign and through his zeal that the translation of the Jewish Scriptures was produced and deemed worthy of a place in the libraries of Alexandria.

But it is time to let our author speak for himself in his own words.

[Extracts from the Letter here follow.]

(15) CHRYSOSTOM, *Homilies on St. Matthew*, V. 2.

The Seventy may justly be deemed more trustworthy than the rest of the translators. The others translated after the coming of Christ, continuing to be Jews, and might with justice be suspected of having spoken rather from enmity and of obscuring the prophecies of set purpose. But the Seventy, in that they approached their task[1] a hundred or more years before the coming of Christ[2] and were so many, are above all such suspicion, and by reason of their date, their number and their agreement may well deserve the greater credence.

(16) EPIPHANIUS, *On Weights and Measures*, 3–11.

[This diffuse and diverting account—in his credulity Epiphanius is like another Herodotus among the Egyptian priests—is interspersed with references, here omitted, to the later Greek versions of Aquila, etc., and to the symbols used in Origen's *Hexapla*. The portions enclosed in brackets ( ) occur only in the Syriac Version edited by Lagarde.]

3 They were seventy-two in number and were shut up from morn till eve in the Pharian island, in the *region*

[1] With a slight emendation we might read "in that they came to the same result" (*i. e.* produced identical versions).

[2] In his *Homilies on Genesis*, IV. 4, he puts the translation under "a certain King Ptolemy not many years before the coming of Christ." Other dates mentioned are 230 B.C. (ps.-Athanasius, *Synopsis*), 31 B.C. (ps.-Theodoret), and 301 B.C. (Nicetas, *Catena on the Psalms*).

called the upper country,[1] over against Alexandria, in six and thirty cells, one pair in each cell. At even they would cross over in thirty-six skiffs to the palace of Ptolemy Philadelphus and feast with him. They slept in pairs in thirty-six bed-chambers. Such was the life they led, to the end that they should have no collusion with each other and should produce an unadulterated translation. The thirty-six cells which I mentioned were erected by the aforesaid Ptolemy in the island across the water. He made them in two compartments[2] and shut in the men two and two, as I said; and he shut in with them two ministering attendants to cook and to wait upon them, and they had shorthand writers[3] in addition. He did not so much as make windows in the walls of those cells, but had what are called "skylights"[4] opened in the roofs above their heads. So they lived from morn till eve under lock and key and so they translated. To each pair one book was delivered, that is to say, the book of the Genesis of the world to one pair, the Exodus of the children of Israel to a second pair, Leviticus to a third, and so on. Thus were translated the scriptural and canonical[5] books, twenty-seven in all, or twenty-two if the reckoning is made to correspond to the number of letters in the Hebrew alphabet. . . .

. . . Thus then were translated these seven and 5
twenty books, also reckoned as two and twenty. They included the Psalter and the additional matter in Jeremiah, I mean his Lamentations and the Epistles of

[1] Cf. Arist. § 301, "the northern district."

[2] Gr. "double."

[3] Or "ready scribes." For Greek shorthand see Milligan, *N.T. Documents*, Note C.

[4] Cf. Arist. § 307, "brilliant light," lit. "down-shining."

[5] Lit. "in the testament."

Baruch; although with the Hebrews the Epistles find no place and the book of Lamentations is the only writing attached to Jeremiah. The method was as already described: the books were distributed periodically to each pair of translators, passing from the first pair to the second, and again from the second to the third in rotation.[1] Thus each book was translated thirty-six times; such is the story which is told. There were also twenty-two of the apocryphal books.[2]

6 When the work was completed, the king took his seat on a lofty throne, and thirty-six readers (sat at his feet[3]) having the thirty-six reproductions of each book, while one held a copy of the Hebrew volume. Then one reader recited and the rest diligently attended; and there was found (no) discrepancy *between the translations*, but a marvellous act of God, that it might be known that it was through the possession of the gift of the Holy Spirit that those men agreed in their interpretation. And where they added a word, they all added it in common, and where they omitted the omission was made by all alike; of the omitted portions there is no need, but of the additions there is need. . . .

9 We must now sketch the plot of the story which is told.[4] A knowledge of these matters will be profitable to thee; the narrative here attempted[5] will indicate who each translator[6] was and whence he came, his date and nationality and the reason why he became a translator. The first to translate this same[7] Holy Scripture from

[1] Text emended. [2] Contrast p. 114 below.

[3] Or "on low stools."

[4] Or "of the events of which we have spoken." He proceeds to describe, out of order, and probably from another source, the preliminary events which led up to the translation.

[5] Meaning uncertain.

[6] The later translators are included as well as the LXX.

[7] Text uncertain.

Hebrew into Greek were seventy-two in number, who produced this same[1] primitive translation under Ptolemy Philadelphus. They were selected from the twelve tribes of Israel, six men from each tribe, as Aristaeus related in his published work. (And their names are as follows :—

Of the first, from the tribe of Reubel[2] :—
Jose, Hezekiah, Zechariah, Johanan, Hezekiah, Elisha.
Of the second, from the tribe of Simeon :—
Judah, Simeon, Samuel, Adai,[3] Mattithah, Salmai.
Of the third, from the tribe of Levi : —
Nehemiah, Joseph, Theodosius, Basa, Orniah, Daki.
Of the fourth, from the tribe of Judah :—
Jonathan, Abrai,[4] Elisha, Hananiah, Zechariah, Hilkiah.[5]
Of the fifth, from the tribe of Issachar :—
Isaac, Jacob, Jeshua, Sambat, Simeon, Levi.
Of the sixth, from the tribe of Zebulun :—
Judah, Joseph, Simeon, Zechariah, Samuel, Salmai.
Of the seventh, from the tribe of Gad :—
Sambat, Zedekiah, Jacob, Isaac, Jesse, Matthi.
Of the eighth, from the tribe of Asher :—
Theodosius, Jason, Jeshua, Theodotus, Johanan, Jonathan.
Of the ninth, from the tribe of Dan :—
Theophilus, Abram, Arsam, Jason, Endemiah Daniel.

[1] Text uncertain.
[2] Another form of Reuben used by Josephus (Roubelos).
[3] Or Adi. [4] Or Abri.
[5] This name has dropped out of all the Aristeas MSS.

Of the tenth, from the tribe of Naphthali :—

Eremiah, Eliezer, Zechariah, Baniah, Elisha, Dathai.[1]

Of the eleventh, from the tribe of Joseph :—

Samuel, Josephus, Judah, Jonathan, Caleb, Dositheus.

Of the twelfth, from the tribe of Benjamin :—

Isaelus, Johanan, Theodosius, Arsam, Avitus,[2] Ezekiel.

These are the names of the seventy-two translators before mentioned.)

Now the successor of the first Ptolemy and the second of the kings of Alexandria was, as we said, Ptolemy surnamed Philadelphus. He was a lover of all that is beautiful and of literature, and built a library in that same city of Alexander in the Bruchium so-called (now an uninhabited district in the said city), which he placed under the charge of one Demetrius the Phalarene. Him he bade collect the books in existence in every quarter of the world, and he wrote letters importuning every king and governor on earth to send ungrudgingly the books (that were within his realm or government); I mean the works of poets and prose writers, orators[3] and sophists, physicians, professors of medicine, historians and so on. One day, when the business was proceeding apace and the books were being assembled from all quarters, the king asked his librarian how many volumes had (already) been collected in the library. He made answer to the king and said: "There are already fifty-four thousand eight hundred, more or less. But I[4] hear that there is still a great mass *of writings* in the world, among the Ethiopians and Indians, the Persians and Elamites and Babylonians, the Assyrians and Chaldaeans,

[1] Or Dathi.
[2] Or Abitus.
[3] Or "rhetoricians."
[4] Gr. "we."

among the Romans also and the Phoenicians, the Syrians and the (Romans)[1] in Hellas." They were not as yet called Romans but Latins. "There are, moreover, with them of Jerusalem and Judaea certain divine books of the prophets, which tell of God and the creation of the world and contain all other teaching that is for the general good. Wherefore, O king, if it is thy Majesty's pleasure to send for these also, do thou write to the doctors in Jerusalem, and they will send them to thee, that so thou mayest lay up the self-same books in the self-same library of thy Reverence." Thereupon the king wrote a letter as follows:—

"King Ptolemy to the (doctors) of the Jews in 10
Jerusalem many greetings. I have built a library and collected a multitude of books from each nation and stored them therein. And hearing that with you also there are current[2] certain books of prophets which tell of God and the creation of the world, and being earnestly desirous to consecrate them with the rest, I am writing to bid you send these to us. That my earnest desire in such a suit is prompted not by idle curiosity or malice but by a regard for *their* honour, and that this request of mine is made to shew my good faith and friendship towards you, you will recognize if you call to mind the benevolence which we shewed to you (on a former occasion). You remember, I ween, how that, when many had been taken captives from your country and had been brought into our country of Egypt, I let them go and dismissed them free, with abundance of supplies, after taking thought for them with no ordinary care; insomuch that I healed those among them who were

[1] Added in the Syriac text; with this reading Hellas apparently stands for Magna Graecia. The Greek has "and them of Hellas."
[2] Or "And hearing a report that there are with you also."

stricken and (likewise) let them go, and the naked did I clothe. And now too I am sending a golden table adorned with the most costly precious stones, of a hundred talents weight, in the room of the table that was taken from the holy place *at* Jerusalem, with gifts and votive treasures[1] for the sacred place. I have recounted these things that ye may know that it is with pious aspiration[2] that I ask for the books."

So the letter was despatched and the gifts (likewise). And they, when they received the letter (and read it) and beheld the gifts, were filled with exceeding great joy. And without delay they had transcribed in Hebrew characters of gold the books which I have already enumerated, two and twenty canonical and seventy-two[3] apocryphal, and sent them off. The king on receiving them looked into them and, being unable to read what was written in Hebrew characters and in the Hebrew tongue, was constrained to write a second letter to them and to ask for interpreters capable of rendering for him the Hebrew into Greek. The contents of the letter were as follows:—

11 "King Ptolemy to the doctors of piety that are in Jerusalem many greetings. 'Treasure that is hid and a fountain that is sealed, what profit is in these twain?'[4] Even so are the contents of the books which ye have sent us. For, since we are unable to read what ye have sent us, it profiteth us nothing. Deign then to send us interpreters, such (among you) as (from early youth) have been accurately trained in the languages of both Hebrews and Greeks."

[1] Or "heirlooms."
[2] Or "in accordance with a vow of piety." Text uncertain.
[3] Contrast p. 110 above.
[4] Ecclus. xx. 30 with Cant. iv. 12 LXX.

Then the doctors of the Hebrews selected and sent the seventy-two translators (before mentioned), following the example of what Moses did aforetime, when he went up into the mount by command of the Lord and heard *the injunction*, "Take with thee seventy men and go up into the mount."[1] But this man,[2] to preserve peace between the tribes, lest, if he took five men from some and six from others, he should create faction among them, devised rather to take seventy-two and to add to the number. In the self-same manner then, as I said, they despatched these men also, who translated the books in the Pharian island so called, as we have related above. And so the books were rendered into Greek and deposited in the first library which was built in the Bruchium. . . .

[After a reference to the daughter library in the Serapeum and the succession of the Ptolemies the Syriac adds :—]

(It was in the days of Ptolemy Philadelphus, in his seventh year, more or less, that the aforesaid seventy-two interpreters translated the books.)

(17) Jerome.

(a) *Preface to the Pentateuch.*

I know not who was the first lying author to construct the seventy cells at Alexandria, in which they were separated and yet all wrote the same words, whereas Aristeas, one of the bodyguard[3] of the said Ptolemy, and long after him Josephus have said nothing of the sort, but write that they were assembled in a single hall[4] and conferred together,[5] not that they prophesied. For

[1] Exod. xxiv. 1 (paraphrased).
[2] Or "he"; *i.e.* the Chief Rabbi.
[3] Jerome uses the Greek word *hyperaspistes*.
[4] Lat. "basilica."
[5] Cf. Arist. § 302.

it is one thing to be a prophet, another to be an interpreter.

(b) *Commentary on Ezekiel*, II. 5 (Ezek. v. 12).

Yet Aristeas and Josephus and the whole Jewish school assert that only the five books of Moses were translated by the Seventy.

[Notwithstanding Jerome's sane criticism above, not many years later Augustine, in his *De civitate dei*, XVIII. 42, is found repeating the legend of the separate cells and the miraculous consensus of the inspired translators. He adds one noteworthy remark, viz. that "the custom has now become prevalent of calling their translation the Septuagint."]

LIST OF THE PTOLEMIES

	B.C.
Ptolemy I, Soter	305–285
Ptolemy II, Philadelphus	285–247
Ptolemy III, Euergetes	247–222
Ptolemy IV, Philopator	222–205
Ptolemy V, Epiphanes	205–182
Ptolemy VI, Eupator	182
Ptolemy VII, Philometor	182–146
Ptolemy VIII, Philopator Neos	146
Ptolemy IX, Euergetes II or Physkon	146–117
Cleopatra III and her sons— Ptolemy X, Philometor II or Soter II or Lathyrus, and Ptolemy XI, Alexander	117–81
Berenike III and Ptolemy XII, Alexander II	81
Ptolemy XIII, Auletes	81–52
Cleopatra VI, her brothers Ptolemy XIV and Ptolemy XV and her son Cæsarion	51–30

NOTE on page 90 (7)

(Contributed by Canon Box)

"THERE seems to be a mixture here of older and later *halakoth.* It seems to me that in its original form the passage referred merely to *script,* not to language. In this case, 'nor in the Median language nor in Greek' will be a later addition, unless these words refer to script. It is interesting to notice that 'in any tongue' is omitted in the best texts. Thus in its original form it would have run probably:—

"'The Law must not be written in ordinary (old) Hebrew script nor in Aramaic (Syriac) script [nor in the Median (v.l. "Elamitic") *language* nor in the Greek *language*]. A copy written [in any foreign tongue or] in any foreign characters (reading כתבים) shall not be used in the service, but only one written in the Assyrian characters.'

"It is curious to note that in *Megilla* 18*a* a reference is made to the book of Esther being read in 'Elamitic.'"